Answering the Tough Ones

Answering the Tough Ones

by
David A. DeWitt

MOODY PRESS
CHICAGO

All Scripture quotations, except those noted otherwise, are from the *New American Standard Bible,* © 1960, 1962, 1963, 1968, 1971, 1972, 1973, 1975, and 1977 by the Lockman Foundation, and are used by permission.

Library of Congress Cataloging in Publication Data

DeWitt, David A
   Answering the tough ones.

   1. Apologetics — 20th century.   I.   Title.
BT1102.D39   230   80-16345
ISBN 0-8024-8971-0

10 11 12 Printing/BC/Year 87

Printed in the United States of America

Contents

Foreword

Large meetings and standardized materials are today's most-often-used means of winning people to Christ. The first sometimes falsely relieve the believer of his personal responsibility for witnessing; the second often fail when the unbeliever raises questions not covered by the packaged approach.

Answering the Tough Ones is unique. David A. DeWitt provides answers to twelve basic questions often asked by unbelievers. These answers are developed from the viewpoint of the unbeliever's doubts, rather than being hints to help the believer "win the argument." The author helps us get inside the mind of the unbeliever so that we can see what he is thinking and therefore be able honestly and openly to help him.

Mr. DeWitt is fully qualified to write this book. The material has grown out of his own ministry in "friendship evangelism" as a regional director of Search Ministries, which seeks to reach unbelievers in nonthreatening, home situations. His theological training (Th.M., Dallas Theological Seminary) and his continual involvement in evangelism make the book biblically accurate and eminently practical.

I hope many of Mr. DeWitt's readers will use his book to help their unsaved friends.

Charles C. Ryrie

Introduction

"Could you be wrong?" Joe asked as he sipped a cup of coffee. His half-open eyes were trying both to examine me and screen out the steam from his coffee at the same time. "I mean about Jesus — could you be wrong about Jesus being God and all that?"

As my mind scanned the evening's events, I wondered if Joe was asking an honest question. Our group had just completed an exciting discussion about life and God.

And it was quite a group! About seventy people had packed themselves into one of Baltimore's nicest homes. There were Catholics, Protestants of various denominations, some Jewish people, and several agnostics. There were also some who believed in reincarnation — one told me he remembered my being a saloon keeper in Baghdad 2,000 years ago!

Joe (not his real name) cornered me at the coffeepot after the discussion. We had barely exchanged introductions when he asked me if I could be wrong about a statement I had made claiming that Jesus was God.

"Sure," I answered.

"Really?" His head jerked back. I wondered whether it was because of my answer or the hot coffee he had just swallowed. Joe's next question convinced me it was not the coffee.

"How about the Bible? Could you be wrong about it being God's Word?" He straightened into a posture that seemed to

11

say, "I dare you to answer that one." His eyes, wide open now, examined me like those of a trial lawyer. I wondered if the answer I had in mind would get me into trouble, but I barged ahead anyway.

"Of course I could be wrong about the Bible," I said. "Everything we know begins with some sort of faith. So, no one can be absolutely sure he's right." I paused to gauge Joe's response.

Because the Februrary weather made the coffeepot corner a crowded place, Joe and I made our way back into the living room while we talked.

"You know something?" Joe continued as we sat down on an empty sofa. "I've never met a Christian who would admit that he could be wrong. I'm an evolutionist," he went on, "and I've decided that Jesus was wrong and so is the Bible. What do you think about that?"

Our Lord had a way of encouraging communication by answering a question with a question. So I tried it. "Tell me something, Joe. Could *you* be wrong — I mean about Jesus and the Bible? Could you be wrong about Jesus *not* being God and the Bible *not* being God's Word?"

Joe's expression froze. Apparently caught off guard, he sat silent, his coffee cup leaning between his fingers and his teeth. After a few seconds he answered, "Well . . . uh . . . of course, I *could* be wrong. As you say, nobody can be absolutely sure he's right . . ." His voice trailed off.

"Well, then," I suggested, "if *I* could be wrong and *you* could be wrong, are you willing to look at this with me and see if we can figure out what's right?"

Before we were finished, Joe invited me to have dinner with him and his wife. We set a date. After several exciting discussions, both Joe and his wife received Jesus Christ as their personal Savior.

I recognized again that something almost mysterious happens in people when they are willing to consider the real issues. But first they must be assured that *we* are also willing to look at both sides.

When someone is open and receptive to the gospel, it may be easy to lead him to Christ. But what do you do when the person is not at that point? Do you forget him and go on to somebody else? That may not be so easy when the person is your husband or wife, son or daughter, mother or father, business partner, or someone else very close to you. What *can* be done to reach him when life's abrasions have left him scarred and hardened to the gospel?

Jesus spoke of four soils into which the Word is sown like seed (Matthew 13:1-15, Mark 4:1-12, and Luke 8:4-10). The soils, of course, are the hearts of people. If their hearts are well-prepared when we present the gospel, they may receive the Lord immediately and grow spiritually. If the soil is not ready to receive the seed, then it must first be softened. We should never compromise the Word, but we *should* cultivate the soil. Years of witnessing to all sorts of hearts have led us to an effective soil-softening idea.

The objective is simple. In talking with people, we attempt to get on their side of the issue and look at their questions as though they were our own.

It is tempting to build a wall of arguments, brick by brick, then offer comments that make the wall thicker. That, in turn, invites the person with whom we are talking to build up his side of the wall. The better the arguments, the thicker the wall between us. To avoid that result, we have endeavored to jump over the wall and work with others from *their* side.

From such a perspective we present twelve basic questions

about Christianity. Since 1971 I have worked with a group of Dallas Theological Seminary students and alumni, plus several nonseminarians. We have worked out, used, and reworked answers to those twelve questions. The chapters that follow contain not merely facts, but chisels designed to chip away at the wall from the honest doubter's side.

This is basically a book for Christians, designed as a tool for use in "softening the soil" of the doubting heart. Each chapter is a journey into the thoughts of some unbeliever. All the conversations are real, reported as they actually happened. I have changed the names and edited the conversations to include questions that deal with the particular topic of each chapter. Many of those discussions are still in progress at the time of this writing. Some of those people, like Joe, have received the Lord Jesus as their personal Savior. Some, however, are still in the process of getting through their wall of doubts.

I hope I have provided not only a tool for the growing believer but also one that he may pass along to a friend trying to cope with any of these twelve questions.

1 • Is Jesus Christ the Only Way to God?

Flight 409 from Dallas to Birmingham was as crowded as usual. Familiar with his tendency to wilt in midafternoon, Tom was planning to snooze a little on the plane before his evening meeting in Birmingham.

As he settled in next to the window, a tall, slim college-age girl took the aisle seat next to him. They exchanged greetings as she wrestled an overstuffed bag into the space under her seat. Leaning back, Tom closed his eyes and tried to doze off. He kept his eyes closed until they began their take-off roll. Then he looked out the window just in time to see the ground drop from under them. Dallas became smaller and smaller and finally disappeared as they poked a hole in the cloud layer that made a ceiling over east Texas.

Tom did not always feel compelled to talk to the people he sat next to on a plane. But this time he was definitely convicted to give this girl a chance to talk about Christ. His guilt was temporarily relieved when he hesitatingly peeled himself away from the window to glance over at her. She appeared to be sound asleep. What a relief! ''Well, God,'' he prayed, ''if You want me to talk with this girl about Jesus Christ, *You* wake her up.''

He had barely finished his prayer, dumping the responsibility on God, when the stewardess plowed into the back of the girl's chair, throwing her forward so hard she almost hit the bulkhead.

"Good morning," Tom said with a grin.

"Really!" She grinned back. "Well, I guess I'm not going to be able to get any sleep."

"My name is Tom," he offered. "What's yours?"

"Jan," she returned. As she put her seat back in an upright position, she asked, "You going to Birmingham?"

"Yep," he answered. "You, too?"

"Uh-huh."

"What for?" he inquired.

"I'm getting married tomorrow," she answered with a big smile that betrayed her excitement — though she was striving for composure.

"Congratulations," he offered. "Tell me about the groom." That, of course, flipped on her "favorite topic" switch. She told him about Jim. He was a football player for the University of Alabama, and they both had one year of college left. After only a few minutes, Tom got the distinct impression Jim could walk on water.

She seemed to feel self-conscious rambling on about Jim, because after a short time she stopped rather abruptly and asked Tom why he was going to Birmingham. He told her he was leading a discussion about the Bible.

"Really!" She seemed pleasantly surprised. "Would you mind if I asked you a question?"

"Not at all."

"Well," she continued, "Jim and I are trying to decide whether to go to church or not. We're not very religious, but we can see the need of establishing roots in some church. Frankly, though, we have a serious question about Christianity. How come Christians act like they have a hotline to God? We've had opportunities to know some couples from several other religions, and they are really neat people who are sincere about their faith. Can you actually say two-thirds of the world's population is going to hell when many of them are more sincere than most Christians?''

"Sincerity," Tom began, "is a very admirable trait, but it doesn't determine truth. I remember a *Peanuts* cartoon where Charlie Brown is lamenting the fact that they have just lost twenty-seven baseball games in a row. In the last frame he turns and looks back at the empty baseball field and says, 'How can we lose when we're so sincere?' Sincerity does not change reality.''

"But aren't all religions working toward the same goal of getting to God?" Jan insisted. "Don't they just use a different path up life's mountain to get there? Mohammed, Buddha, and Krishna all claimed to be or to have ways to God, but none of them were exclusive about it.''

"Jesus," Tom answered, "did not just claim to be the only way to God. He claimed to *be* God. *If* God had inspired several key people of the world like Mohammed, Buddha, Krishna, and Jesus, and then we came along and claimed Jesus is the only one that's any good, that would be unfair.''

"Right. That's what I mean." Jan nodded.

"But," he continued, "that's not the case. The Bible teaches that God Himself became man in Jesus of Nazareth and died for everybody all over the world — including Mohammed, Buddha, and Krishna. Is there anything unfair about God doing that?''

"No, I suppose not," Jan answered cautiously, "but what makes Christians so narrow-minded? I'm not sure I want anything to do with a God who would encourage His people to be so narrow and exclusive.''

"Truth," Tom answered, "is always narrow. I want this airplane to have a narrow-minded pilot. I want him landing

only at airports that are big enough. Besides that, I want him
landing on the runway at the airport, not between the runways
or in the parking lot. That's narrow, but it's not bad, because
it's right.''

"It just seems condescending, intolerant, and unloving to
go around telling people that they're going to hell if they
don't believe like you do,'' Jan persisted.

"Do you believe in polio vaccinations?'' Tom asked. "I
mean, do you believe that everybody ought to get themsleves
and their children vaccinated?''

"Sure.''

"Isn't that condescending, intolerant, unloving, and narrow?''

"Yes — No! — But that's different,'' Jan insisted.

"Not if both are really true.''

"But Christians sure do turn a lot of people off.''

"Oh,'' Tom agreed, "a person can be obnoxious with the
truth. It is not good to be repulsive about anything, but that
doesn't stop the truth from being narrow.''

"It doesn't bother me if others believe in Christ,'' Jan
claimed, "as long as they don't tell me and everybody else
that we have to do that too. Even if I believe that Christ is true
for me, that does not mean He has to be true for the rest of the
world.''

"But, you see, Jan, that's not the case when you are
dealing with objective truth. That's OK if we are talking
about our own individual feelings and opinions, but not when
we are considering facts.''

"I think I'm starting to get your point,'' Jan answered. "If
Jesus was right, that would really make a difference.''

"Yes,'' Tom continued. "Suppose I told you, 'I believe
this airplane will get us to Birmingham.' If you said, 'That
may be true for *you*,' I'd disagree. It's not true for me unless

it's true for everybody on board.''

"But what about other planes to Birmingham? Couldn't Jesus be *a* way to God without being the only way?''

"The trouble is," Tom answered, "that would mean what He did say is not true, and the opposite of what He said *is* true. It seems to me we'd be starting a new religion. It would not be Christianity, since we would be decidedly contradicting Christ.''

THE ONLY WAY TO HEAVEN

Tom and Jan discussed five different aspects to this question. Let's take a minute to think them through.

1. IS IT ENOUGH TO BE SINCERE?

Although sincerity is an admirable quality, to sincerely follow something that is wrong is to be sincerely wrong. Sincerity does not change reality.

During my undergraduate days at Michigan State University, we had an unusual snowstorm. Normally, Michigan snow is rather damp and forms solid snowdrifts that will pretty well hold you up when you jump into them. One particular storm, however, lasted for three days and left very dry, powdery snow almost up to the second-story windows of some dorms. Lots of kids thought it would be great fun to jump into that huge snowdrift from the third- and fourth-floor windows — having all the confidence in the world that it would hold them up.

It didn't.

We had students in nearly every class with broken legs from jumping out windows. One guy on our floor who hurt his leg in basketball even wore a sign around his neck: I Did Not Jump into the Snow.

Now, those kids were sincere. They had so much conviction that the snow would hold them up that they jumped out the window. Now that is sincere faith! They not only believed it, they also acted on their faith. Only problem is — they were wrong! The same thing is true in religion. No matter how many people believe it and regardless of how sincere they are, if they are wrong, the results can be disastrous.

2. WHAT IS THE DIFFERENCE BETWEEN CHRISTIANITY AND THE OTHER RELIGIONS?

In a sense, nearly all founders of the major world religions claimed to be ways or have ways to get to God (though they all defined God differently). But Jesus claimed to *be* God. Many non-Christians find it difficult to believe that a man (Jesus) could become God; but that is not what happened. The Bible teaches that *God became man* in the form of Jesus of Nazareth — not the other way around.

The reason He took on humanity was so He could die — in place of Mohammed, Buddha, you, and me. Jesus said that He came "to give His life a ransom for [the Greek word literally means "as a substitute for"] many" (Matthew 20:28).

3. AREN'T CHRISTIANS TOO NARROW-MINDED?

People are often quick to recognize that Christianity is intolerant of other beliefs. That is true. But the reason is that Christianity emphasizes objective truth. That is, it is based on real history — real people, places, and events. Christianity is basically news, not views. Truth is narrow by definition. Tolerance in personal opinions is a virtue, but tolerance when dealing with facts is ridiculous.

4. IS IT UNREASONABLE TO SAY, "THAT'S OK FOR YOU BUT NOT ME"?

Anything that is true objectively and universally cannot be applied only privately. If it is true, then it is true for everybody, and if it is not, then it is not true for anybody.

I shall always remember a large, loud, elderly, lady math teacher I once had. I can still hear her bellowing: "Remember, DeWitt, if you don't come up with the same answer that I have, either you're wrong or I'm wrong, but we can't both be right!'' If Jesus said that He is the only way to God, and Mohammed or anybody else said that there is some other way to God, then either Jesus is wrong or Mohammed is wrong. They cannot both be right.

Jesus said, "I am the way, and the truth, and the life; no one comes to the Father, but through Me" (John 14:6). Before this, He said, "I and the Father are one" (John 10:30). He went on to say, "He who has seen Me has seen the Father" (John 14:9). Either He is the only way to God the Father, or he is not. If He is, then that is true for you and me as well as everybody else, no matter where they live or what they believe. If He is not, then it is no more true for me than for anybody else, no matter how much I believe it.

5. COULD JESUS BE ONE OF MANY WAYS TO GOD?

To claim Jesus is just one of many ways to God is to say the opposite of what *He* said. If that were true, He would be wrong. If His basic message is wrong, then He is not a reliable way to anything. His claim to be the only way was not just a sidelight; it was the heart of His whole message. He was the only way because He was God, the Creator of the universe (John 1:1-3; Colossians 1:16-17). So if there is any other way, then His basic message is wrong and He is not a way at all.

WHAT ABOUT JAN?

Let us look back in on Tom and Jan for a minute.

Their DC-9 began its descent into Birmingham. As the seatbelt light came on, Tom asked Jan if she had ever made the decision to invite Jesus Christ into her life as God. She said she had not. Next, he asked her if there was anything standing in the way of her receiving Christ as her Savior right

then. Before the wheels touched the runway, she prayed with
him to invite Jesus Christ into her life. He gave her some
verses to read to Jim and encouraged her to invite him to
receive Christ, too. Tom said good-bye to her as they got off
the plane.

About a year later, Tom got a letter from Jan. She had had
some good discussions about Christ with her new husband,
which resulted in his receiving Jesus Christ as his God and
Savior. They had gotten involved in a Bible-oriented church
and seemed to be growing in the Lord. Tom told me, ''I've
never heard from her since, but I look forward to seeing her
and meeting Jim in heaven some day.''

2 • Are Miracles Possible?

He called himself Orange. It must have been because of his bushy crop of reddish orange hair — though nobody ever asked. Jay talked to him only one time and never learned his real name, but he would never forget their conversation.

Orange was an enthusiastic go-getter in his midtwenties, eager to inform everyone around him of two facts: he was an atheist, and he was a seminary student. In all fairness to the seminary, a liberal one on the East Coast, Orange claimed he went there to escape the draft (back when it was possible to do that). Beneath his superficial atheism seemed to beat a sincere heart of true atheism. He embraced a genuine pity for people who went to seminaries that were narrow-minded enough to teach the Bible as true.

Orange, along with six of his anti-religious friends, showed up at a discussion party about life and God led by Jay in a majestic old home in the central area of Memphis. Orange and company added significantly to the discussion. Their opinions were welcomed by the Christians and applauded by some non-Christians twice their age. The lively confusion produced several people looking for answers; as well as Jay could recall, four of them received Christ — one was a guy who came with Orange.

After the discussion was over, Jay talked with several people, working his way toward the dessert table. He ran into

Orange next to the punch bowl. Having done so much talking during the discussion, they felt like old friends.

"Say, Orange," Jay began, "tell me something. What would God have to do to prove to you that He existed?"

"I want to see an angel," he answered without the slightest hesitation, "a twenty-foot-tall angel, shining in brilliant green, standing right here in this room, pointing his finger at me, and saying, *'Orange, the Bible is true!'* "

"Really?"

"Really!"

"How come you don't think the Bible is true?" Jay inquired.

"Because it's full of fairy tales."

"You mean miracles?" Jay asked.

"Yeah. Why don't I see any miracles? Where's my twenty-foot, shining, green angel?"

The ceiling of the room where Orange pointed seemed almost twenty feet high, so Jay proceeded as if he were serious. "OK, Orange," he agreed. "Let's suppose you saw a twenty-foot-tall, shining, green angel right now pointing his finger at you, saying, *'Orange, the Bible is true!'* What would you conclude? Be honest, now."

"I'd conclude somebody spiked the punch!" Orange chuckled.

"Exactly," Jay continued. "I appreciate your honesty. But then don't tell me that's what God needs to do to make you believe in Him."

"I suppose you have a point," Orange admitted. "But it seems to me the people who saw Jesus do miracles had an easier time believing than we do."

"That may be true," Jay answered. "The miracles often served as a sort of catalyst to help people believe, but that's not why they occurred."

"Then why *did* they occur?"

"They authenticated what God was doing," Jay explained, "but they didn't create faith. Jesus claimed to be God. His miracles were important because they were something anybody could see as evidence that He was not lying or having delusions of grandeur. They were not done to generate faith in people who had already decided that He was wrong."

Orange and Jay consumed enough punch to satisfy a thirsty camel. It seemed the more they talked, the more they drank. Fortunately, it was made just out of fruit juices and some sort of carbonated soda. When the hostess arrived to refill the punch bowl, they decided it was time to stop making pigs (or camels) of themselves and leave the dining room. The room with the snack table adjoined a huge foyer which had, among other things, a stairway reminding Jay of the front of some capitol building. It led to a landing and then branched into two stairways that circled up to the next floor. Jay and Orange perched themselves on the fourth step and resumed their conversation.

"If the miracles of the Bible are for real," Orange went on, "why weren't they recorded in history, and why don't we observe that sort of thing in science?"

"I assume you mean natural history and the natural sciences?" Jay asked.

"Uh-huh," Orange grunted, propping his elbows on the step behind him.

"Well, by definition natural history and the natural sciences include only things that are observable today. Christ's miracles are not. When natural historians or scientists consider the miracles recorded in the Bible, they immediately put them in the category of something other than natural history or natural science. Therefore, they do not accept them as data pertinent to their field of study — so, obviously, we don't find them there. We don't conclude that dinosaurs never existed simply because we don't find any at the zoo. The zoo is a collection of living animals, not extinct ones. If we are going to determine whether or not miracles existed as recorded in the Bible, we must ask ourselves if it is reasonable for *those* events to have heppened at *that* time.''

"You mean the Bible doesn't say there are supposed to be miracles today?'' Orange asked.

"First, we have to define what we mean by miracles,'' Jay suggested. "The Bible says God answers prayer and gives direction to the lives of those who seek Him. If we call those things miracles, then God does miracles today. But suppose we define miracles as events contrary to the nature of our three-dimensional universe — like walking on water and crossing the Red Sea on dry land. The Bible nowhere says that you and I should expect to see these in our daily lives. Most of the people in Bible times didn't see any of those events either.''

By this time they had attracted an audience. Six or eight people had gathered around just to listen in. Some sat on the empty steps below. Others leaned on the wooden railing. One guy even walked between Orange and Jay, though it seemed to Jay there was plenty of room to go around, and positioned himself on one of the steps above them. Jay felt a little like a Christian facing a lion in the arena of ancient Rome. Orange was well aware of the fact that he was now on stage, but that did not slow him up at all.

"I have people tell me that they see miracles every day,'' Orange continued. "They talk about the birth of a baby and the beauty of a flower, and then conclude that the whole world is full of miracles. That seems dishonest to me. They are avoiding the real issue. If those things are examples of what they mean by miracles, then they don't believe in miracles any more than I do. Isn't it being deceptive to say you believe in the supernatural miracles of the Bible and then prove it by telling me about babies and flowers?''

"Oh, yes," Jay agreed. "There are two ways to destroy the concept of miracles. One is to say there are no such things. The other is to say everything is a miracle. If everything is a miracle, then nothing is. So the real question becomes, 'Is it reasonable for contrary-to-nature events to have occurred or not?'

"If there is a God," Jay continued, "then He can do miracles. A supernatural being is capable of supernatural activity. If you don't believe there is a God, then maybe we should talk about that first.''

"No. I want to hear your answer to the miracles question," Orange decided. "Let's assume there is some sort of God and go from there.''

"All right," Jay continued. "The word *miracle,* in one sense, is a relative term. A miracle for one type of being might not be a miracle for another.''

"So what you are saying," Orange concluded, "is that if there is another type of being beyond man in the universe, then he could do things that would seem miraculous to us.''

"Exactly," Jay continued. "And not only that, but if that being were an infinite creator, it would be 'natural' for Him to command dimensions far beyond the three we observe. That would make very reasonable the occurrence of events that are miraculous to us.''

MIRACLES ARE FOR REAL

The question of miracles is much more crucial for Christianity than for the non-Christian religions, In other faiths, miracles can be disbelieved without affecting the message of the religion itself. In Christianity that is not the case. "If Christ has not been raised," Paul explains, "your faith is worthless; you are still in your sins" (1 Corinthians 15:17). If there were no such things as miracles, the other world religions would remain essentially unchanged. But Christ's resurrection requires a Christian's belief in miracles.

Contrary-to-nature events are central to establishing Christianity as true. If there are no such things as miracles, then there was no resurrection of Jesus Christ from the dead, and Christianity is a waste of time. In his book *Miracles,* C.S. Lewis writes, "All the essentials of Hinduism would, I think, remain unimpaired if you subtracted the miraculous, and the same is almost true of Muhammadanism, but you cannot do that with Christianity. It is precisely the story of a great Miracle. A naturalistic Christianity leaves out all that is specifically Christian."[1]

During their brief discussion, Orange asked five different questions:

1. DO MIRACLES PRODUCE FAITH?

Orange essentially wanted to know why God does not perform more miracles — assuming that, if He did, there would be more believers. But the purpose of miracles is not to produce faith. When Jesus raised Lazarus from the dead, the Bible says some believed. But it also says, "the chief priests took counsel that they might put Lazarus to death also; because on account of him many of the Jews were going away, and were believing in Jesus" (John 12:10-11). Acts 4:16-17 records that the same thing happened when Peter and John healed the lame beggar. Jesus Himself said, "If they do not listen to Moses and the Prophets [that is, the Bible], neither will they be persuaded if someone rises from the dead" (Luke 16:31).

If someone is willing to decide to believe, then a miracle

could help him decide more quickly or easily. Lighter fluid may help your charcoal burn more readily. But lighter fluid will not start the fire. And if someone is predisposed not to believe, then no amount of miracles will create faith.

The reason God provided miracles was to authenticate that a particular message or messenger was indeed from Himself. After the author of Hebrews wrote, "How shall we escape if we neglect so great a salvation?" he went on to say, "After it was at the first spoken through the Lord, it was confirmed to us by those who heard, God also bearing witness with them, both by signs and wonders and by various miracles and by gifts of the Holy Spirit according to His own will" (Hebrews 2:3-4). The miracles verified that the great message of salvation was indeed from God.

2. WHY DO WE NOT FIND MIRACLES IN SCIENCE AND HISTORY?

Science and history deal with that which is "natural" to our universe as we observe it today. Miracles are not natural; so by definition they are not part of the study of natural science or natural history. As Jay mentioned, the occurrence of miracles does not depend on our observing them in nature, any more than the existence of dinosaurs depends on our observing them at the zoo. The question is, If we had scientifically recorded facts and history as we observed the life of Jesus of Nazareth, would we have observed what the eyewitnesses of that day claimed to have seen? The question is not, Do you see dinosaurs today? but rather, Would you have seen them then?

3. SHOULD WE EXPECT TO SEE MIRACLES TODAY?

The Bible does not claim that all people, whether they lived in Bible times or are alive today, should expect to observe contrary-to-nature events. The fact that something happened does not mean it ought to happen to everyone. God does not expect all of us to cross the Red Sea on dry land like the Israelites or walk on water like Peter did. For that matter, most of the people living in Bible times and places did not see any miracles either. Actually, miracles were most prominent at three points in history: the times of Moses and the children of Israel, Elijah and the prophets, and Christ and the apostles. But even at those periods, most of the people (even the ones who genuinely believed in God) never saw any miracles.

4. IS LIFE FULL OF MIRACLES?

People commonly refer to wonders of nature as "miracles." But that only confuses the issue by using two different meanings for the word "miracle." Saying everything is a miracle destroys the concept of miracles as effectively as saying there are no such things. Certainly, there are wonders of nature that cause us to marvel at God's handiwork. But those are natural not *super*natural. The Bible also describes some events that are beyond the nature we observe every day. Those *are* supernatural. When we say we believe in miracles and then refer to the birth of a baby or the beauty of a flower, we are illustrating the supernatural with the natural — thus denying the existence of anything beyond the natural.

5. HOW DID SUPERNATURAL MIRACLES HAPPEN?

How miracles happened was the final question Jay and Orange considered. The answer, of course, is that they were the normal act of a supernatural being. What is unreasonable for a human being in a three-dimensional universe might be commonplace to a creator controlling more than three dimensions.

An example comes to mind from my old days as a math teacher. Much of mathematics is designed around two dimensions instead of three. Let's call it flatland. Imagine a place like a flat tabletop, except spread out all over the room and beyond. If I, a three-dimensional being, took a bowling ball and passed it through the plane, the event would appear as several miracles to the flatlanders. First, a dot would appear. Then it would become a circle. It would get bigger, and then smaller, as I passed the ball through the plane. Finally, it would make a dot again and then disappear. Now flatlanders know dots cannot appear from nowhere. They do not become circles and then dots again by themselves. What is their explanation? It was a miracle. But if they understand that I exist in a dimension beyond theirs, what happened is not unreasonable. In the same way, if there is an all-sovereign, creating God controlling all the dimensions beyond the three we live in, it would be reasonable for Him to penetrate our world with the miraculous events described in the Bible.

A MIRACULOUS PERSPECTIVE

A word of caution is in order here. In answering the question about miracles, it is crucial to maintain a truly biblical viewpoint. Many try to get the Bible off the hook by explaining away the miracles in some way other than supernatural occurrences. Some try to say the stories of Adam and Eve or Jonah and the whale are myths rather than actual historical events. Or they may claim that the wind blew the Red Sea back in a spot shallow enough for the Israelites to cross. That kind of thinking is clearly in conflict with the plain, normal interpretation of the Scriptures. More understanding of our three-dimensional universe may unravel some of the reasoning behind the wonders of nature, but it will never give natural explanations for the supernatural events recorded in the Bible.

Then there are some who believe God is performing supernatural events today, and they mention that to the unbeliever. The problem is, those events are probably outside the experience of the unbeliever asking about miracles. All it does, therefore, is widen the communication gap between the two of you. Besides that, present-day miracles are not the real issue. A person needs to receive Jesus Christ as his or her God and Savior; and that message comes from the Bible, not from today's activity. Therefore it is the Bible, not current events, with which an unbeliever must deal as his source of truth. A defense of modern experience adds nothing to that.

What is my advice? Do not apologize for the Bible as understood in a normal sense. Do not add modern miracles to dazzle your unbelieving friends with your experience. Just "make a defense" (1 Peter 3:15) for the truth God's Word contains.

WHAT ABOUT ORANGE?

The group of people that gathered around Jay and Orange began to ask both of them questions. Before long what had been a personal discussion became a public forum, which continued until it was time to go. Jay had only a short time to talk with Orange alone just before they left. Orange was still a long way from Christ, but he said he had thought that question through much more clearly than before. Many people like him come to Christ when they have the opportunity to "reason" with someone concerning the truth of the Word of God (see Acts 17:2-4).

NOTES

1. C.S. Lewis, *Miracles* (New York: Macmillan, 1947), p. 83.

3 • Can Anyone Be Sure He's Going to Heaven?

"I can't talk with my mother about it," Lisa said to Kay. "She just gets upset and mopes around the house getting me depressed. I wish she'd go back to Chicago. I'm going to die. I've come to accept that. My cancer is terminal, and that's that. But I want to face death squarely and openly, you know what I mean?"

Kay nodded. But, of course, she did *not* know what Lisa meant. Kay had never faced death, at least not in the way Lisa was facing it now, knowing she probably had less than a year.

As they walked quietly across the yard, they relived some pieces of their friendship. It was not far from Kay's yard to Lisa's, but the way was lined with memories. They passed Lisa's flower bed. It was the one that caused, or should I say forced, them to meet when Lisa had asked Kay to keep her boys from running all over her roses. Then there was that spot on the sidewalk where Lisa's husband first told Kay that Lisa had terminal cancer.

In all this Kay tried to find a way to tell her new friend about her faith in Jesus Christ. But it was awkward. Not just because Lisa was dying — they talked freely about that. But how could she bring up the subject of salvation? The two neighbor couples had gone out to dinner several times. After Lisa's surgery, Kay had bought her a new nightgown. Some days Kay just knocked on Lisa's door before going to the store to see if there was anything she could get her. And when Lisa was up and around, they had gone to lunch together. Generally, both talked impulsively, rattling on about who knows what. But today Lisa seemed quiet and thoughtful. They went into her house and got themselves glasses of iced tea.

"Kay," Lisa asked, staring blindly into her glass of tea, "do you think I'm good enough to get into heaven?"

"Honey, it's not a matter of being good," Kay answered. "It only depends on believing in Jesus Christ as your Savior."

"I know," Lisa continued. "But what if I stop believing? Aren't there Christians who believe for a while and then stop?"

"I'm sure there are," Kay answered. "It's certainly possible to stop believing and start doubting. But God's gift of eternal life isn't like that. It doesn't depend on what we do. After we receive it, we can't give it back."

"But gifts *can* be given back."

"Only some kinds," Kay continued. "A while back I gave you a new nightgown. You could give that back all right. But suppose I had given you a polio vaccination, and later you stopped believing that vaccinations did any good. Could you give it back?"

"I see what you mean," Lisa mumbled into her tea.

"And the Bible says eternal life in Christ is just that kind of gift."

"But I just know He's going to ask me about some of the awful things I've done," Lisa insisted.

"Let me ask you this," Kay went on. "How many sins did Jesus pay for when He died on the cross?"

"All of them, I guess."

"And when you receive Christ, that payment is applied to you, isn't it?"

"I guess so," Lisa answered with uncertainty.

"Well, then, when you accept Christ, all your sins are paid for," Kay explained, "all you've done and all you ever will do."

"But how do you know God's gift is really like that?" Lisa asked.

"The Bible says it was written 'to you who believe in the name of the Son of God, in order that you may *know* that you have eternal life' [1 John 5:13]. It never says anything about maintaining eternal life. Anything eternal is unable to end. Since we get this eternal life when we 'believe in the name of the Son of God,' it is something we have now, not just later. So if we have eternal life now, we couldn't possibly lose it later, or it wouldn't be eternal."

"So you think God will let me into heaven no matter what I've done?" Lisa inquired.

"I don't think a person's getting into heaven has anything to do with what she's done. Saving people from their sinful condition is work, all right, but God did all the work. If you receive Him, then your getting into heaven depends on Him, not you. The question is not, Are you good enough? but, Was Jesus Christ good enough?"

CAN YOU BE SURE ABOUT HEAVEN?

Lisa and Kay talked about four separate questions that surrounded this topic. Let's look at them a bit closer.

1. DO YOU STOP HAVING ETERNAL LIFE WHEN YOU STOP BELIEVING?

It is possible, of course, for Christians to stop believing. I suppose every Christian stops believing God at some time or other. Maybe even several times a day. But what is usually assumed is that those who stop believing also stop being saved — and that is contrary to the Bible. The apostle Peter tells us we are "born again . . . to obtain an inheritance which is imperishable and undefiled and *will not fade away,* reserved in heaven for you" (1 Peter 1:3-4, italics added).

Suppose you make a decision to get on an airplane to Chicago, then after you are on board you stop believing in airplanes. Are you going to get to Chicago or not? Getting there does not depend on your ongoing belief or the absence of it. It depends on the airplane. In the same way, once we have received Christ, our eternal life depends on God and not on our ongoing faith.

Speaking about those who believed in Him, Jesus said, "I give eternal life to them, and they shall never perish; and no one shall snatch them out of My hand" (John 10:28). Christ said *no one,* not *no one except ourselves.* We can stop believing, but we cannot stop being eternally saved. Salvation from sin is the kind of gift that cannot be returned — like the polio vaccination Kay mentioned to Lisa.

2. WHAT ABOUT THOSE SINS WE HAVE COMMITTED AFTER RECEIVING CHRIST?

Can we be assured God will not ask us about sins committed after deciding to trust Christ? The answer lies in an understanding of what happened when Jesus died on the cross. The Bible, speaking of Christ's death, says "through *one act of righteousness* there resulted justification of life to *all* men" (Romans 5:18, italics added). "All men" includes lots of men who were not even born. Yet their sins were paid for, too. Christ's death on the cross paid for all the sins of all time, not only the ones that had happened up to that time. When we receive Him as our own Savior, He applies that payment to us. So all our future sins are just as paid for as our past ones — even our sins of disbelief.

3. CAN WE BE ASSURED OF ALWAYS HAVING A RELATIONSHIP WITH GOD?

Eternal life is not *eternal* life unless it *is* eternal. Jesus said, "He who believes in the Son has *eternal* life" (John 3:36, italics added). But He went on to explain that that eternal life begins not when we get to heaven but as soon as we receive Him as our Savior (John 5:24). Now either Jesus was telling the truth or He wasn't. And if He was, then those who receive Him have a salvation that is *eternal* from that point on.

4. ARE WE ABLE TO MAINTAIN OUR RELATIONSHIP WITH GOD?

Our salvation is based on God's ability, not ours. "He saved us," Paul told Titus, "not on the basis of deeds which we have done in righteousness, but according to *His* mercy, by the washing of regeneration" (Titus 3:5, italics added). In other words, *God* did the saving. It is not something we do anything to get or keep. We simply receive it.

When my daughters were very small, each like to hold my finger in her hand, but I held her whole hand with my fingers. When she fell, as she inevitably did, she could not hold my finger tightly enough to keep herself from falling. But I held onto *her* hand tightly enough to keep her up. The fact that she did not fall depended on me, not her. Sometimes she even wanted to fall, but I would not let her. So it is with God. He does not keep us from stumbling or even from rebelling and wanting to fall, but He does keep us from falling out of our eternal relationship with Himself. When we receive Him, we become "children of God" (John 1:12). When I became a child of my parents, I could decide to be a good child or a bad child, but I could never lose my position as a child in my family.

WHAT ABOUT LISA?

Kay sensed that Lisa was not a Christian; that is, she had

never personally received Christ. Kay was right. Often when people have trouble being sure of their position with God, they are not real believers. The Bible says, "The Spirit Himself bears witness with our spirit that we are children of God" (Romans 8:16). Kay could not see any of that inward confirmation from God in Lisa's life. It is important to understand that although we *can* have assurance of our salvation, we should not be in a hurry to give that assurance to people who still do not show the leading of God's Spirit in their lives after a long time. "For," Paul writes, "all who are being led by the Spirit of God, *these* are sons of God" (Romans 8:14, italics added).

Lisa and her husband began going to a Bible-teaching church. After many other conversations with Kay and various people from that church, Lisa received Jesus Christ as her own personal Savior. Her husband also accepted Christ during that time.

One day Lisa came over to Kay's house all excited about her decision to accept Christ. "All the things you told me are so clear now," she said. "It's like giant blinders have been taken off my understanding."

Two months later Lisa went home to be with the Lord Jesus Christ whom she had come to know and love.

4 • Is the Bible Reliable?

It was one of those lazy spots in the middle of the afternoon. Mike found himself studying the tops of the buildings visible from his law office window instead of finishing the letter he was working on. It had been the usual busy day for a lawyer: depositions, a court appearance, a bunch of letters and phone calls. But now his mind was drifting.

It was time for a break.

Taking his coffee cup and some papers on archaeology and the Bible he wanted to photocopy, Mike headed for the snack room, which housed both the coffeepot and the copy machine.

The only other person in the room was Jerry, one of Mike's law partners. He was smoking a cigarette and thumbing through a magazine. They exchanged the usual polite acknowledgements of each other's presence while Mike started the machine on its task of clunking out the copies he needed.

"What are you copying?" Jerry asked.

"Some stuff that proves the Bible is reliable," Mike answered.

"How does it do that?"

"It shows that people like Abraham's great-great-great-grandfather and places like Jerusalem actually existed way back around 2400 B.C. when the Bible says they did."

"But," Jerry questioned, "how do you know the Bible is

accurate? It sure doesn't seem like it would be. It was written by biased people who wanted to promote their faith. These guys could have made mistakes like anybody else. Besides that, it's been translated so many times, how do you know it's still the same? You know how information gets all mixed up when you pass it on from one person to the next. Haven't you ever played one of those games where you pass a message around a circle and it comes back so different you can't even recognize it?''

"I really don't know the answers to all those questions," Mike admitted.

"Then how can you believe that the Bible is accurate?" Jerry wanted to know.

"Well, for one thing," Mike answered, "I know it's accurate because it's accurate. I mean, I just showed you evidence that it is. *However* it got here, here it is! And it always checks out to be right. You have not proved the Bible is inaccurate just because it seems like it ought to be. The question is, 'What does the evidence say?' ''

"Archaeology only covers certain specific things in the Bible," Jerry insisted. "Couldn't it still be wrong in some of the spots you can't check out?"

"Could be," Mike agreed. "But since everything we *can* check out shows it to be right, it would be more logical to assume the rest of it is. If we were to treat it like a civil lawsuit, we would ask, 'What does the preponderance of evidence show to be true?' ''

Jerry wasn't satisfied, so he asked, "Since the Bible was translated from Hebrew to Greek to Latin to German to whatever and finally to English, don't you think we've lost something somewhere?''

"I'd think so if the English Bible *was* the end of a long succession of translations like that, but it's not.''

"It's not? Whaddaya mean?"

"I mean, the Old Testament was written in Hebrew, except for a bit of Aramaic, and the New Testament in Greek. The English Bible I have on my desk was translated directly from those original languages, not from any other ones in between."

Jerry seemed surprised by that new information. He sat thoughtful for a minute, then asked, "You said there was lots of different evidence — what's something else?"

"Well, let's see," Mike said, taking his papers out of the copy machine. "One thing that comes to mind is its consistency and unity. It was written over a period of fifteen hundred years by about forty different people, and yet it has the same thing to say from cover to cover — and about controversial issues, too."

Then Mike got himself a cup of coffee and sat down at the table. Since Jerry seemed to be soaking in everything, Mike kept on talking. "Besides that, there's fulfilled prophecy. About one-quarter of the Bible was unfulfilled prophecy at the time it was written. And everything that it said would happen by now, has come true."

Mike paused for a minute while he sipped on his coffee, then said, "Another thing that must be considered is that the Bible claims to be inspired — "

"Objection, Your Honor!" Jerry interrupted. "That's circular reasoning. You can't use the Bible's own claims as proof of its accuracy."

"It's self-testimony, and self-testimony is valid evidence — objection overruled!"

"Even so," Jerry insisted, "how do you know that those early church councils that put the Bible together got the right books in it?"

"Those councils didn't really decide which books were

going to *be* included,'' Mike explained. ''They merely observed that God was using certain books and not others in the
lives of believers. They put *those* together in one unit that we
call the Bible. Actually, God Himself, using those books in
the lives of people, is the One who pointed to the books that
should be included.''

''Even if all that is true,'' Mike's partner persisted, ''I
don't know how we could possibly tell what it means. Look
at all the different denominations and cults that disagree with
each other, and all of them claim to be following the Bible.
How could you possibly know the right interpretation?''

''The main issue,'' said Mike, ''is whether you want to
follow what the Bible says or use it to prove what you already
think ought to be true. Cults are groups following something
other than the Bible — like some special leader or some new
'revelation.' With denominations, it's a little different.
Within nearly every denomination you have those who believe the Bible is literally God's Word and those who don't.
Those who don't are really using themselves as an authority.
But those who believe it is literally God's Word use pretty
much the same principles of interpretation.''

''What do you mean by 'literal'?'' Jerry asked. ''Do you
mean to tell me you believe there are four corners on the
earth?''

''No more than I believe Jesus is a piece of wood hanging
on hinges because He said He was the 'door,' '' Mike answered. ''Those are figures of speech. By literal I mean
plain, ordinary, normal, regular, just reading the Bible the
way you'd read any literature. You and I use the term 'sunrise' all the time. The sun doesn't actually rise; the earth
rotates. But we know exactly what we mean without quibbl-
ing over precise astronomical terms.''

RELYING ON THE BIBLE

Let us break away from Mike and Jerry for a few minutes. They continued to talk the rest of the afternoon about all kinds of Bible-related topics. But it might be helpful to fill in some details of the seven areas they have already touched on. They are:

1. WHAT DOES ARCHAEOLOGY SAY ABOUT THE BIBLE?

Archaeology has become one of the most helpful areas of study for demonstrating the Bible's reliability. The point is simply that the people, places, and events mentioned in the Bible do coincide with what we know archaeologically about those same people, places, and events. Nelson Glueck, a Jewish archaeologist, in his book *Rivers in the Desert: History of Neteg* put it this way: "It may be stated categorically that no archaeological discovery has ever controverted a biblical reference."[1]

An example of one such discovery is the one Mike mentioned. It was made by two Italian scientists at Ebla in Northern Syria. A *Time* magazine article reported, "Their discovery does more than provide documentary evidence of a little-known kingdom that existed between 2400 and 2250 B.C.; it also provides the best evidence to date that some of the people described in the Old Testament actually existed."[2]

A trip to any Christian bookstore can provide several volumes of archaeological materials that show the Bible is in agreement with history.

2. HAS THE BIBLE LOST ITS RELIABILITY THROUGH RE-TRANSLATIONS?

A second area deals with the trustworthiness of the manuscripts from which we get our English Bible. There is a common misconception that our English Bible sits at the end of a long chain of translations and retranslations of the original. That's just not so.

How *did* we get our Bible? Well, let us look at the origin of the New Testament. After it was written, it was copied by professionally-trained men. Then those copies were copied, and so on until the introduction of the printing press around 1500. Today we still have about five thousand of those early copies. Some are just fragments, others are very complete, but none of them are translations from one language into another. They are copies made in the same language — Greek. In addition, there are around nine thousand others that were made in different languages (mostly Latin). All the copies can be compared to reproduce an accurate Greek New Testament. The English translations we use come directly from the Greek — the same language in which the New Testament was written.

3. WHY IS THE BIBLE CONSISTENT?

A third very awesome fact that Mike pointed out is the Bible's consistency. It was written over a period of fifteen hundred years in sixty-six different volumes by about forty different authors using three different languages (Hebrew, Greek, and a little Aramaic) writing on three different continents (Europe, Asia, and North Africa), and yet each part has the same things to say about life's most controversial issues.

Also, the authors came from widely varied backgrounds. Moses was a well-educated political leader. Joshua was a general. Solomon was a king. Daniel was a prime minister. Nehemiah was a cupbearer. Amos was a herdsman. Peter was a fisherman. Matthew was a tax collector. Paul was a teacher — a rabbi. It is completely unlikely that those men would have the same things to say unless one and the same God inspired them to write down each word without any errors.

I offer consistency as evidence for the reliability of the Bible because people just do not agree that easily. Even in more objective subjects like physics, chemistry, medicine, or dentistry, people do not agree! Try comparing medical books written over fifteen hundred years to determine how to cure a stomachache. The chemistry books from which I learned "facts" in high school are full of things we "know" are not true today. No doubt if we ask any two people — in the same profession in the same office who know each other — to write on the same subject, we would note numerous areas of diagreement.

Actually, if we could sit down with all the writers of the Bible and talk with them, we would probably find differing opinions and ideas just like any other group. Therefore it is unlikely that the writers wrote the Bible on their own. *But!* When they picked up their pens to write the material we have in the Bible, using their own very different personalities, they still wrote things in complete accord with one another. The most likely explanation is the one the apostle Peter gave when he wrote, "Men moved by the Holy Spirit spoke from God" (2 Peter 1:21).

4. HOW ACCURATE ARE THE BIBLE'S PREDICTIONS ABOUT THE FUTURE?

A fourth piece of evidence is biblical prophecy. The Old Testament gives scores of predictions of what would happen to certain nations, cities, and people, *all* of which happened or are happening just the way the Bible said. Babylon, Persian, Greece, and Rome all rose and fell the way the book of Daniel said they would. The city of Tyre was destroyed just as Ezekiel 26 predicted. The book of Genesis records God's promise to Abraham that his descendants would never be wiped out; today the Jews and Arabs, descendants of Abraham's first two children, Isaac and Ishmael, are still with us — as distinct peoples. There are no Babylonians today. There are no Medes or Persians, no Amorites or

Canaanites. God told Abraham:

>And I will make you a great nation,
>And I will bless you.
>And make your name great;
>And so you shall be a blessing;
>And I will bless those who bless you,
>And the one who curses you I will curse.
>
>Genesis 12:2-3

The most casual look at history shows that those nations who have "cursed" the Jewish people no longer exist, all the way from the ancient Assyrians to the modern Third Reich of Adolf Hitler. Yet the Jews continue.

There are several hundred prophecies pointing to the coming of the Messiah that were perfectly fulfilled in Jesus Christ. Some of those are: the place of His birth (Micah 5:2 and Matthew 2:1), that He was to be born of one called a virgin (Isaiah 7:14 and Matthew 1:23), His life-style as a suffering servant (Isaiah 53), His triumphal entry into Jerusalem on the colt of a donkey (Zechariah 9:9 and Matthew 21:4-11), the betrayal for thirty pieces of silver (Zechariah 11:12 and Matthew 26:15), His humble attitude at His trial (Isaiah 53:7 and Matthew 27:11-14), the piercing of His hands and His feet (Psalm 22:16 and Matthew 27:35), His being beaten and spit upon (Isaiah 50:6 and Matthew 26:67), the gall and vinegar they gave Him to drink while on the cross (Psalm 69:21 and Matthew 27:34), the casting of lots for His clothing at the crucifixion (Psalm 22:18 and Matthew 27:35), the burial (Isaiah 53:9 and John 20:28), and that He was to be called God (Isaiah 9:6 and John 4:25-26).

5. WHAT DOES THE BIBLE CLAIM ABOUT ITSELF?

Jerry, you recall, objected to circular reasoning — using the Bible to prove the Bible. But we are talking about evidence, not proof; and because, after all, the Bible is on trial in a question like this, we should hear what it says about itself. Self-testimony *is* valid evidence.

The Old Testament authors often make statements like "And the Lord spoke to me, saying," or, "The word of the Lord came unto me saying." Henry Morris in his book *Many Infallible Proofs* claims there are 2,600 such claims of inspiration in the Old Testament.[3]

The New Testament is no less specific in claiming an every-word accuracy for both itself and the Old Testament. Jesus said, "For truly I say to you, until heaven and earth pass away, not the smallest letter or stroke shall pass away from the Law, until all is accomplished" (Matthew 5:18). While quoting what, humanly speaking, Moses wrote in the Old Testament, Jesus called it what "God said" (Matthew 15:4). Peter equated the apostle Paul's writings with "the rest of the Scriptures" in 2 Peter 3:16, and he wrote, "For no prophecy was ever made by an act of human will, but men moved by the Holy Spirit spoke from God" (2 Peter 1:21). And in 2 Timothy 3:16, Paul told Timothy, "All Scripture is inspired by God."

So the authors of the Bible claimed not only that they were speaking from God, but that the other biblical writers were, too. In other words, if we conclude that the Bible is not inspired by God word-for-word, then we are saying that Moses, David, Peter, Paul, and Jesus Christ were wrong — and that we know more about the Bible than they did.

6. WERE THE RIGHT BOOKS INCLUDED IN THE BIBLE?

What if those church councils left some out or included some wrong books? The main point here is that the church councils did *not* determine what books should be in the Bible. *God* did that by using certain writings in the lives of His people. Athanasius in A.D. 367 listed the twenty-seven books now in our New Testament as the ones God was obviously using.[4] A little later Jerome and Augustine did the same.[5] Church councils only *recognized* what God was already doing. Cairns, in his book *Christianity Through the Centuries,* says, "Later councils, such as that at Chalcedon in 451, merely approved and gave uniform expression to what was already an accomplished fact generally accepted by the Church for a long period of time."[6] But notice — that was done after God had already preserved those books over three hundred years.

As an example of what we are saying, let us suppose we took the Bible apart into its individual books and scattered those volumes around a bookstore. Further suppose that we erased from everyone's memory the fact that they ever were, or ever should be, inspired by God or bound together as God's Word. Twenty years from now, most of the books on the shelves would be different; but those sixty-six would still be there. Publishers would keep reprinting them because people would keep buying them. And the reason they would keep buying them is because God would be using them in a special way in their lives. After a hundred years, they would still be there. And probably even before the three or four hundred years it took the early church to put them together, some publisher would get the idea of bunching those obviously used-of-God books into one volume.

There was another criterion used in double-checking to be sure any particular book should be included in the New Testament. It had to be written or sanctioned by an apostle — one of those twelve (minus Judas, plus Paul) to whom Jesus had spoken directly. Christ Himself told them, "I have many more things to say to you, but you cannot bear them now. But when He, the Spirit of truth, comes, He will guide you into all the truth" (John 16:12-13). Because lots of false teachers arose in the early church, all writings not following the obvious teaching of the twelve apostles were not considered.

7. WHO HAS THE RIGHT INTERPRETATION OF THE BIBLE?

The fact that every group today seems to have its own view, and they all differ, causes confusion.

The answer here is actually quite simple. For the most part, those differing groups are not trying to *interpret* the Bible at all. Instead, they are promoting a set of views connected to the life-style they are living. In order to gain acceptance for that life-style, they attempt to show that the Bible teaches what they already believe. Words and phrases can be lifted out of the Bible and plugged into your own context to sound like you are following the Bible. The same can be done with any book, of course. If *Poor Richard's Almanac* were as popular a source of authority as the Bible, no doubt most groups would use that to prove their ideas. The only reason they use the Bible is that the Bible is already so widely accepted.

There *are* people within nearly every denomination, however, who *do* want to learn what the Bible has to say, and as a whole they will share the same basic interpretation of the Bible. Even in the few areas of disagreement, they all agree that there must be only one right view.

Here are two principles to be followed by people who want to find out what the Bible says: First, interpret each phrase within its context. Ask what the particular author is talking about. To do that, the reader must consider the historical background surrounding the writing of the book. What was the situation that the author was addressing? Were his readers at war? Were they suffering? Was there apostasy? Then, after something of the historical situation is known, ask what the particular chapter, paragraph, or sentence being interpreted says about the author's general theme and purpose.

The second principle is: take everything at face value. In

other words, do not spiritualize the passage until you have first understood its most obvious intent. I call that taking it literally. What I mean by that is taking it in a plain, ordinary, normal way, the same way you would read a newspaper. A man once asked me how I would interpret him if he said, "My heart bleeds." We had been discussing this subject, and he was looking for a way to prove that I really could not tell what he meant. If I said he had an emotional problem, he would say he meant that he had a physical one. If I said he had a physical problem, he would say he meant that he had an emotional one. So I told him it depended on what else he said. "If you wrote a letter to me," I answered, "and told me you just flunked your final exams at college, your girlfriend left you, you just lost your job, and your heart bleeds, I'd assume you had an emotional problem. But if you wrote that you just had open-heart surgery, had fallen out of bed and rolled down the stairs, were coughing blood, and your heart bleeds, I'd assume you have a physical problem."

Taking things at face value requires knowing what kind of literature you are dealing with. A factual description must be understood differently from a figure of speech. The Bible contains poetry, prophecy, parables, and visions as well as narratives and history. It is important not to take metaphors, similes, and the picturesque language of poetry as a description of history (such as the "four corners of the earth"). But it is also important not to take historical events surrounding Adam and Eve or Noah and the Flood as just myths or stories.

WHATEVER HAPPENED TO JERRY?

Mike and Jerry talked for several hours that afternoon. They locked up the office and went down the elevator still talking about the Bible. Before they parted to go home, Mike asked Jerry to receive Jesus Chirst as his personal Savior. But

Jerry said he was not ready. At the time of this writing, the conversations are still going on in that law office. Although Mike tells me he feels that Jerry is getting closer, he has not yet accepted Christ.

NOTES

1. Nelson Glueck, *Rivers in the Desert: History of Neteg* (Philadelphia: Jewish Publication Soc. of Amer. 1969), p. 31.
2. Hedley Donovan, ed., "A New 'Third World,' " *Time,* 18 October 1976, p. 63.
3. Henry Morris, *Many Infallible Proofs* (San Diego: Creation Life, 1974), pp. 156-57.
4. Earle E. Cairns, *Christianity Through the Centuries* (Grand Rapids: Zondervan, 1954), p. 128.
5. Ibid., pp. 155-61.
6. Ibid., p. 128.

5 ● Isn't Just Believing Too Simple?

"Lori, will you shut the light off and go to sleep?" Bob pulled his blanket over his head, but his muffled voice continued scolding his wife from beneath the covers. "For Pete's sake. You gonna read that dumb book all night?"

"Oh, don't be such a grouch," Lori returned, realizing that Bob's gruff voice also had humor in it. "Besides, it's not a dumb book!"

"Probably a silly novel," Bob teased.

"It's about Charles Manson and all the people he had murdered."

"Beautiful! Great bedtime reading," Bob said with comical false sarcasm. Then a thought hit him. Maybe God was giving him an opportunity to witness to Lori. He had prayed that his wife would receive Christ ever since he had done so two years before. They had had several good discussions, but as yet she could not see why she needed to receive Christ. So, instead of complaining, he poked his head out from under the covers and asked, "Do you think Manson could ever go to heaven?"

"Of course not!" Lori answered, and then added, "Do you?"

"I think there's one way."

"How?"

"If he received Jesus Christ as his Savior."

"That's crazy," Lori said.

"Why?"

"Because it's just too easy. Getting someone like Charles Manson to heaven just can't be that simple."

"Oh, I didn't say it would be *easy* to get him to heaven. I *am* saying it would be simply a matter of his receiving Christ."

"What's the difference?" Lori asked.

"It was hard for God to pay the price for Charles Manson's sin, just as it was hard for Him to pay the price for all our sins. God the Father sent His Son to become the man Jesus of Nazareth, who was rejected, beaten, nailed to a cross, killed, and separated from the Father just to pay for our sins. Now that's not easy! It's also true that nothing is free, including the price of getting people to heaven. But once the payment is made and eternal life is offered as a gift, then it's free and easily received."

"But I'm not as bad as Manson," Lori pointed out.

"No, but the cost of getting you and me to heaven is still too high for *us* to pay."

"Yes, but I'm basically a good person," Lori went on.

"Yeah. Compared to a mass murderer — but not compared to God. And it's God that's doing the judging, not Manson. The Bible says, 'THERE IS NONE WHO DOES GOOD, THERE IS NOT EVEN ONE' [Romans 3:12] and that 'all have sinned and fall short of the glory of God' [Romans 3:23]."

"All right," Lori conceded. "But it seems too easy for someone to just believe in Christ without doing anything else."

"The thing is," continued Bob, "some things are only available as a gift. Suppose I wanted my own eighteen-hole golf course. The only way I'd ever get it is for somebody else to pay for it and offer it to me as a gift. Either I'd receive it, which would seem easy to me, or I'd never have it. But either way, it cost the *buyer* a fortune. Because something is free doesn't mean it's cheap.''

EXPENSIVE BUT FREE

Bob and Lori discussed two separate questions within this issue. They are:

1. ISN'T IT TOO EASY FOR PEOPLE TO GET TO HEAVEN BY SIMPLY RECEIVING CHRIST?

Someone like Lori, who is struggling with the concept of salvation as a gift, realizes everything has a price tag. It certainly seems unreasonable that people like Charles Manson, Adolf Hitler, and Jim Jones should get off scot-free by just believing in Christ. We can certainly agree with Lori about that. Nobody has his sins erased by believing. The point is — Jesus Christ, being God, paid the price for those sins in full (2 Corinthians 5:21; Romans 5:18). That was not easy! How easy would it be for you to send your only child to die for someone else's crimes? Lori is right. It takes a lot more than belief. But now that our sin is paid for completely, and that payment resulting in eternal life is offered by God as a gift, it can be *received*.

2. WHY SHOULD VERY BAD PEOPLE GO TO HEAVEN AS EASILY AS GOOD PEOPLE?

Those stuck on the question of wicked people's "so easily'' going to heaven must be helped to realize that they, too, are in need of Christ's payment and that they cannot earn salvation themselves. The Bible says, "All our righteous deeds are like a filthy garment'' (Isaiah 64:6), "THERE IS NONE RIGHTEOUS, NOT EVEN ONE'' (Romans 3:10), and "The wages of sin is death, but the free gift of God is eternal life in Christ Jesus our Lord'' (Romans 6:23). We must help people realize that we cannot do the work that pays the price for our sins. Some things are like that. We could not do the work necessary to perform our own brain surgery, no matter how much we needed it done. It would have to be carried out by someone else. The mechanics of signing the paper allowing the surgeon to do it might be easy, but that does not mean the surgery would be easy to do or worthless to have done. At times it is not a good idea to reject something just because it is free and easy to receive, and the Bible says salvation is like that.

WHAT ABOUT LORI?

Bob and Lori stayed up talking until about 2:00 A.M., when she received Jesus Christ as her own God and Savior. They have gone on to be an exciting couple still growing in the Lord together.

Did you notice how Bob did not insensitively preach at her? Neither did he come on condescendingly toward her views. He recognized the opportunity that God made for him.

But what allowed him to make use of that God-given opportunity was the positive relationship he already had with his wife. His jokes about her reading arose from his acceptance of her, which kept their communication open.

We need to approach people like the apostle Paul, who reminded the Thessalonians, "We proved to be gentle among you, as a nursing mother tenderly cares for her own children" (1 Thessalonians 2:7).

6 • What About Those Who Have Never Heard?

"Do your kids like milk or Kool-Aid?" asked Pam, juggling a milk carton and a pitcher of Kool-Aid while shutting the refrigerator door with her elbow.

"Kool-Aid," Nancy said, "but give them milk. They've been eating too much sugar lately."

"Boy, I know what you mean." Pam poured five glasses of milk for her two children and Nancy's three.

Fixing lunch for themselves and the kids had become a several-times-a-week routine for those two.

It was awkward at first. When Nancy moved into the neighborhood, Pam had gone over to meet her. A mutual friend explained that Nancy's husband had been an airline pilot, but he was killed in a hijacking. Since Pam's husband was an airline pilot, too, it seemed she could help, and Nancy — left alone to raise three children in a new neighborhood — needed a friend.

At first Pam wanted nothing more than to be that friend. But as time passed and she came to know Nancy better, she felt a growing desire to talk with her about Jesus Christ.

"That lasagna sure smells good," Pam remarked.

"Oh, it's only leftovers."

"But it still smells good."

"I suppose," Nancy reluctantly agreed. "But I'm sorta getting sick of it."

"Really?"

"Yeah. It seems like I have it at least once a week. I'm in a rut." Nancy went on. "I need to do something different."

"Want to go to a Bible study with me?" Pam asked. She had prayed that somehow she would be able to work that invitation into the conversation. She had not thought it would be so easy.

"I don't think I want to go," Nancy answered. "I don't think the Bible is very fair."

"What makes you say that?"

"Because there are people all over the world who never heard of the Bible, and I don't think any God who would send them all to hell is very fair."

"Well, the Bible says God *is* fair," Pam answered, dealing the exact number of potato chips to each of the five plates — thus averting a war at the table.

"If He's fair, then He'll let everybody into heaven," Nancy persisted.

"I don't know if that's the most fair thing to do or not," Pam returned. "But if it is, that's what He'll do."

"But don't *you* think everybody needs to believe in Jesus?"

"Yes, I do," Pam admitted.

"Then what about those people who live their whole lives completely isolated from Christianity?"

"Well, they can see the wonders of God in nature," Pam suggested, "and they have a conscience that tells them there's a right and wrong. It seems like they'd want to know what sort of God was behind all that."

Their conversation was interrupted by several trips to the picnic table and a summons calling the kids back from ter-

rorizing the neighborhood. Once the five had all been lo-
cated, there was the job of nailing them to their spots around
the picnic table. That was followed by the task of refilling
two glasses of spilled milk, getting them to eat off their own
plates, and answering, "Because I said so," to the com-
plaints of "*Yuk*! Milk! Why do I have to drink this junk?"

Pam was afraid that by the time they got to their lasagna,
Nancy would forget her question. But she didn't.

"Even if isolated people wanted to find God, I don't see
how they could do it," she said as she poured Pam a glass of
iced tea.

Pam answered, "I think God could find some way to tell
people about Jesus if they really wanted to find the way to
God."

"How do you know they're not already worshiping
Jesus?" Nancy asked. "Maybe they are just calling Him a
different name."

"It's not the English name 'Jesus' that's important," Pam
answered. "It's the whole Person. Nobody else I've ever
heard of said what Jesus did. He claimed to be God the Son
and the only way to God the Father. Besides, His basic
message was different from anybody I've ever heard of."

"Why does it just have to be Jesus?" Nancy objected.
"Couldn't God let people who have never heard of Jesus into
heaven another way? I mean, God is all-powerful, isn't He?"

"Sure," Pam agreed.

"Well then, He must be powerful enough to get them in
some way other than telling them about Jesus."

"Yes. But if He is powerful enough to tell them about
Himself without Jesus, then isn't He also powerful enough to
bring them to Himself through Jesus?"

"Then what about babies and insane people who don't

have the ability to decide to believe in Jesus?'' Nancy persisted.

"I really don't know,'' Pam admitted. "But I think the Bible says somewhere that they are going to heaven automatically.''

"Are the people who lived before Jesus going to be sent to hell just because they had the misfortune of being born too soon?''

"No. They have the same chance as the rest of us.''

"How do you figure that?'' Nancy wanted to know.

"Because the God of the Old Testament hasn't changed, and He told them the Messiah would come to pay for their sins. They had just as much opportunity to believe in Jesus looking forward to His coming as we do looking back at it.''

THOSE WHO HAVE NEVER HEARD

Many Christians tend to avoid the problem of those who have not heard by saying, "Don't be concerned about those people over in those primitive areas who have never heard. What about you who *have* heard?'' It is true that "what about those who haven't heard?'' can be a smokescreen put up by an unbeliever to dodge the real issue. I have found, however, especially in talking with adults, that it is usually a sincere question that needs a response.

Their real question is, "What is God like?'' Many people honestly are not sure they want to give their lives to a God who is so mean and uncaring that He sends people to hell just because they have never heard of Him.

Nancy and Pam discussed several aspects of the issue.

1. HOW CAN WE SAY GOD IS FAIR IF HE SENDS TO HELL PEOPLE WHO HAVE NEVER HEARD OF HIM?

Whatever God does, it is going to be fair. But many feel if *that* were true, then He would let everybody into heaven — or at least all the "good" people. Well, because of the reasons given in chapter 8 of this book, we might question whether that would actually be fair. But, if that *is* fair, then that is what He will do.

The Bible rhetorically asks, "Shall not the Judge of all the earth deal justly?" (Genesis 18:25). In other words, the God who judges the whole earth will be just and fair to each individual. Romans 2:11 reads, "For there is no partiality with God." Whatever God does about those who have never heard of Jesus Christ will be the most fair thing to do.

2. WHAT ABOUT PEOPLE WHO HAVE BEEN COMPLETELY ISO-
LATED FROM CHRISTIANITY? HOW CAN THEY RESPOND TO
CHRIST?

Every person, no matter what his geographical location, has at least two sources of information about God to which he can respond.

Nature is one source. As we observe the universe around us, we see design and beauty far beyond anything we or even nature itself could produce. In chapter 12 we deal specifically with natural revelation. What is important to point out here is that everyone has the same natural wonders around him, and they point to a superior being beyond man whom anyone may choose to seek.

If I were to live in your house a while, I would know you existed even if I never met you. The pictures, artifacts, and designs I would find around the house would tell me of your existence as a distinct person with a definite personality. I would have enough information to decide to try to find you if I wanted to. The apostle Paul put it this way: "For since the creation of the world His invisible attributes, His eternal power and divine nature, have been clearly seen, being understood through what has been made, so that they are without excuse" (Romans 1:20).

But nature is not our only source of information about God. Another one is within ourselves — conscience. We have the idea of a standard of goodness beyond what we are able to keep. Conscience tells us about sin: the difference between the way we live and the way we know we ought to live.

A few days ago, I had a man in my office who had been an atheist most of his life. He told me how as a teenager he had rejected the beliefs of the church he grew up in and replaced them with a moral code that he thought he should live by. Then he tried to live by it.

"To my suprise," he told me, "I couldn't keep my own moral standards. What's worse, I found myself *pretending* I was the kind of person I had decided I should be, even though I couldn't pull it off."

"That's fascinating," I said. "You made up your own religion, converted yourself to it, then backslid from it, so you became a hypocrite about it!"

He agreed.

We both had a good laugh. But there is a point here not to be overlooked. Even though he outwardly rejected God, he could not escape his inner knowledge of a goodness beyond what he was able to keep. Speaking of those who have never heard, the Bible says, "They show the work of the Law written in their hearts, their conscience bearing witness, and their thoughts alternately accusing or else defending them" (Romans 2:15). What finally brought him to a belief in God was his realization that man has a sense of goodness far greater than he needs for basic survival.

3. HOW COULD SOMEONE IN AN ISOLATED AREA KNOW ABOUT JESUS CHRIST, EVEN IF HE WANTED TO?

God has obligated Himself to respond to people who respond to Him. When someone looking at nature and his own conscience wants to find the source of the goodness and righteousness within it all, God promises He will reveal Himself to that person.

I have heard it said that Christianity is not a religion, because religion is man seeking God, whereas Christianity is God seeking man. Actually that formula is only partly true. Chirstianity *is* God seeking man; but it is *also* man seeking God. God is seeking those who respond to whatever they can know about Him. Ezekiel wrote, "For thus says the Lord God, 'Behold, I Myself will search for My sheep and seek them out' " (34:11). Jesus said, "For the Son of Man has come to seek and to save that which was lost" (Luke 19:10). But God also wants people to seek Him. Jesus said, "Seek, and you shall find" (Matthew 7:7). Hebrews 11:6 reads, "He is a rewarder of those who seek Him."

Missionary records are filled with stories of people from isolated areas who had no exposure to the Bible or to anyone who knew the message of Christianity, yet were seeking a good, loving God of some kind. God answered their search by leading some missionary to them to tell them about Christ. From Mongolia to the depths of Africa, we hear people saying things like, "I always knew He existed, but I never knew His name," or, "I've always known there was a loving God somewhere."

Some object that a person sincerely seeking God would probably just become a loyal follower of his own tribal religion. Experience does not bear that out. I have not observed true seekers of God turning back to become loyal followers of their childhood religion. Most reject it! The more sincere they are, the more they question. Jesus said we should have the faith of a little child — but every child I talk to about God has gobs of questions! Seeking people generally reject any ideas that are inconsistent with what nature and conscience tell them is right.

4. COULDN'T PEOPLE BE WORSHIPING JESUS BUT CALLING HIM BY A DIFFERENT NAME?

For one thing, I know of no other religion, following the teachings of any other leader, with anywhere near the message Jesus had. On the surface they might *appear* the same. Non-Christian religions have commandments and morals and rules to live by and accept some sort of supernatural being and promote the betterment of man. But while other leaders claimed to be prophets of God or one of many gods, Jesus claimed to *be* God, the only God, the Creator of the universe (John 14:7-9). All non-Christian religions I have studied teach a "works" system of reaching God or becoming better. Jesus taught that no works will get one to God; faith alone accomplishes that (John 5:24; 6:28-29). Most religions point primarily to the betterment of man; Jesus pointed primarily to the glory of God (John 12:44-45). The religions of man may claim to be *a* way or a *better* way, but they generally do not declare themselves the *only* way; Jesus asserted that He was the only way and that there was absolutely no other way (John 8:24).

Besides that, the name of Jesus *is* significant. Christ Himself said that the reason some people would end up being condemned was because they did not believe "in the *name* of the only begotten Son of God" (John 3:18). The Bible says that "at the *name* of Jesus every knee should bow, of those who are in heaven, and on earth" (Philippians 2:10). (See also Acts 5:41, 1 John 3:23 and 5:13, and 3 John 7.) Of course when we say the name of Jesus is significant, we do not mean the English word J-E-S-U-S. We mean the person, the actual carpenter of Nazareth identified by that name. Salvation lies in that individual Man — not in His philosophies or teachings or in the way we pronounce His name, but in Jesus of Nazareth, who was the Creator of the world.

5. COULDN'T THOSE WHO HAVE NEVER HEARD OF JESUS BE LET INTO HEAVEN SOME OTHER WAY?

Still another question is, "After all, if God is completely powerful, then could He not reveal Himself to those isolated people by some way other than telling them about the Jesus of the Bible?"

Of course, God *could* do anything He likes. But we might also ask, "Since God is powerful enough to reveal Himself some way other than how He said He would, then is He not also powerful enough to do it the way He said He would?" God told us very clearly that people come to Him through hearing about Jesus Christ (Romans 10:14). The Bible does not tell us that people can come to God any other way. Therefore, to say there is some other way is to say we know more than the Bible reveals. If God wants to lead people to Himself some other way, that is up to Him. But for *us* to say He might do that goes beyond what the Bible reveals — and God has not given us that assignment.

Then there is the additional problem of how people coming to God any other way could have their sins forgiven. Since all men are sinners (Romans 3:23) and therefore unable to have a relationship with God (Isaiah 59:2), and since Jesus Christ is God's only provision for man's sin (1 John 2:2), there is apparently no other way for people to get to God.

6. WHAT ABOUT BABIES AND INSANE PEOPLE WHO CAN'T BELIEVE IN JESUS?

We admit that it is unusually difficult to find clear biblical teaching about the salvation of infants and the mentally disordered. But we *can* say this: biblical evidence indicates that people unable consciously to choose Christ are not held accountable for rejecting Him.

In 2 Samuel 12:23 David spoke of his infant son, who had just died. He reasoned, "But now he has died; why should I fast? Can I bring him back again? I shall go to him, but he will not return to me." David certainly was a believer and would go to be with God when he died. We can conclude that the baby, though he was never able to believe, was already with God.

Deuteronomy 1:39 reads, "Moreover, your little ones who you said would become a prey, and your sons, who this day have no knowledge of good or evil, shall enter there, and I will give it to them, and they shall possess it." The "it" of that verse is not eternal life; "it" is the promised land of Palestine, not heaven. But the principle is the same. Those who were not able to be accountable were not held accountable.

The rest of the Bible teaches the same. The reason people everywhere are lost is because they are conceived with a sin nature (Romans 5:12). Jesus Christ paid for all sin on the cross (1 John 2:2). But people are still separated from God because they have rejected Christ. They reject Him when they do something they know is wrong. Jesus Christ is the embodiment of all the goodness that man ought to be. To reject Christ is therefore to reject righteousness. But the converse is also true: to reject righteousness (which we do every time we intentionally sin) is to reject Christ. A mentally disordered person never has the ability to reject righteousness. Neither does a baby. But as a normal infant grows up, there comes a point (and the age varies with each individual) when he *does* have within himself the knowledge of good and evil. At that time, his intentional sinning is a rejection of righteousness, which is a rejection of Christ — whether he ever heard of Christ or not. But before that time, he does not have the ability to reject Christ.

Therefore, we can conclude that Scripture indicates that babies and the insane are *not* lost.

7. WHAT ABOUT PEOPLE WHO LIVED BEFORE CHRIST?

God's plan to restore man to a relationship with Himself has never changed. The message of salvation in the Old Testament is the same as in the New. Man is described as a sinner separated from God (Isaiah 59:2) and in need of a redeemer (Job 19:25). The only way people could get to God was by grace (Psalm 6:2) through faith (Genesis 15:6), and not by their own works (Isaiah 64:6). The object of their faith was the personal Messiah (Isaiah 53:5) who would be God Himself (Isaiah 9:6) when He would come to earth as a baby (Isaiah 7:14). They needed to have faith in the Messiah who would come, just as we need to have faith in the Messiah who did come. The details of His coming were revealed progressively. Each age was given more details, and even we who are living today do not see it as clearly as we will when Jesus returns to earth. But the essential message has remained unchanged since God first revealed the need of a sacrifice to Adam and his sons, Cain and Abel.

The magi who came from the East to bring gifts to the baby Jesus were seeking God. As far as we can tell, they had no previous knowledge of God or the Bible. But God led them — not just to general knowledge about Himself, but to the most specific revelation He had ever given: Jesus Christ. And when they knew of Him, they recognized Him as the object of their search. The same is true with those seeking God today. When He leads them to Jesus, they recognize Him as the God they are seeking.

WHAT ABOUT NANCY?

Nancy has not yet accepted Christ as her Savior — though she may by the time you read this book. One of the people I wrote about had not yet received Christ, but when shortly afterwards he did, I went back and changed the end of that chapter. The same may happen to Nancy. Pam is still her close friend and they still get together regularly. Pray that God will use Pam or someone else to lead Nancy into the Kingdom of God's Son.

7 • Isn't Christianity Only a Psychological Crutch?

As Greg drove over the dark back roads of Knoxville, Tennessee, he could not help marveling at the man sitting next to him. It was after 2:00 A.M., an unusual time to be taking someone home from a Bible study. But then Lou was an unusual man, and theirs was an unusual study.

For one thing, the reason Greg was taking him home was because Lou was too drunk to drive. Several Christian friends had been playing tennis and golf with Lou for months before he agreed to come to a study. Then for three or four weeks he made up excuses about why he did not come after he had promised to. Then he said he would come only if he could bring his half-gallon of bourbon and cuss and swear as much as usual. When he finally came, the first thing he said was, "I don't buy this #&$%¢* religious stuff!"

As Greg rolled over the situation in his mind — the study group he was leading, the discussion he had with Lou afterwards, his offer to drive Lou home — he also reviewed for himself some other things he knew. Lou was a lawyer and fairly well off; but he had not always been that way. He had grown up on the streets of New York City, never knowing who his parents were. He stole nearly everything he ate as well as the clothes on his back until he was fifteen years old.

69

Lou's childhood memories were of bouncing from one foster home to another.

When they arrived at his home, Lou invited Greg in to talk some more. As they settled into his living room, Lou began to open up. "If it wasn't for Frank and Charlie, I'd write this whole thing off," Lou said. "Those two used to be the most obnoxious #&$%¢*'s I've ever met. But now they are the most humble, loving men I could ever imagine — and it absolutely blows my mind!" He sat silent for a moment, then added, "It must be a psychological crutch. They probably need some religion to turn it all over to, so they don't have to worry."

"Well," Greg responded, "I'm not trying to tell you how to live your life or anything, but isn't your bottle of bourbon a crutch?"

"Oh, sure," Lou admitted, "but it makes me feel good. That way I don't worry so much."

"Trouble is," Greg went on, "it won't work."

"How do *you* know?"

"Because everybody wants to know who he is and what life's all about. That's just part of being human. But you'll never find that in your bottle. The bourbon is only mental morphine that keeps you from dealing with those real issues about yourself."

"But religion does the same thing!" Lou protested. "Most religious people I know are like zombies that get high on something emotional or traditional and stop thinking. Their religion is like my bourbon. It's what you call 'mental morphine,' and I don't feel any need for that #&$%¢* junk."

"Sure," Greg agreed. "A religious system used as a pain killer isn't any more helpful than booze. But it's too simple to lump off Frank and Charlie as just two guys with a religious background having an emotional experience. Either what they believe is true or it isn't. They believe that Jesus Christ rose from the dead. Their believing it doesn't make it so, but neither does it make it false. If what Jesus said is true, then you and I have a real need for Him even if we don't feel it psychologically.''

MORPHINE OR PENICILLIN

Greg and Lou wrestled with an issue that deserves a thoughtful answer: "If I don't feel any need for a religious psychological crutch, why should I bother with Christianity?" You may know someone with a question similar to that one. Two questions you might help them answer are:

1. WHAT IF I DON'T NEED RELIGION?

Every human being seeks meaning for life. We want to know things like: Who am I? Why am I here? What am I for? Am I significant? Where am I going? Many people in our society (especially males under the age of thirty-five) seem to think they are being "macho" if they say they do not need religion. In reality they are not being "macho," they are just being immature. We can stick our heads in the sand if we wish and say we are not interested in those things; but before long we will find ourselves seeking answers, just as certainly as we will seek food, water, and shelter. Every human society (no matter how educated or primitive) has religion, and it is taught by the most stable, intelligent members as well as the most emotional and unthinking ones. Even the great European psychologist Carl Jung said that all the psychologically ill patients over thirty-five that he had seen were ill because they did not have a healthy religious outlook. If we are to remain mentally healthy, it is not a matter of *if* we will seek those things; it is only a question of *how*.

2. ISN'T RELIGION JUST A CRUTCH FOR PEOPLE WHO WANT TO BELIEVE SOMETHING?

Jesus Christ said, "I am the way, and the truth, and the life; no man comes to the Father, but through Me" (John 14:6). That does not become *true* because I feel like believing it, nor does it become *false* because I feel like not believing it. It is either true or it is not. My believing *can* make me feel better, but that is like morphine. I might *feel* better if I believed the same way about Buddha or Mohammed or my new sportcoat. That is still morphine. I can deaden my nerves so I worry less and have more peace for awhile. But unless it is real, I could actually be getting worse while I think I'm getting better. If Jesus Christ was God and did pay for my sins, and if by receiving Him I can have a relationship with the real Creator of the universe — that's a *cure,* not a crutch! It is penicillin, not morphine! It is an answer and a direction that I need, whether I feel like I need it or not.

REACHING PEOPLE LIKE LOU

Several factors played a part in Lou's openness to the gospel. First, his Christian friends loved him just as he was. They did not condemn him for his life-style. Instead, they brought him to hear the gospel just as he was. God honors that. During Christ's ministry on earth, four friends brought a paralytic to Jesus on a stretcher and lowered him through the roof. It was not the faith of the sick man that got him to Christ, but that of his friends. The Bible says, "And seeing *their* [the friends'] faith, He [Jesus] said, 'Friend, your sins are forgiven you' " (Luke 5:20). The friends did not first require him to be well; and neither, for that matter, did Jesus. It is the same with Lou and many like him. We cannot require that they clean up their lives before we get them to Christ. Jesus wants people to come to Him just as they are.

After sharing a meal and conversation with some people much like Lou, Jesus turned to His critics and said, "It is not those who are healthy who need a physician, but those who are sick; I did not come to call the righteous, but sinners'' (Mark 2:17).

A second thing to notice is how Greg used the testimony of the changed lives of Frank and Charlie. An example of what God has done in someone's life can be very effective, especially in dealing with the "psychological crutch" question. A word of caution, however: a testimony of your experience can be helpful to an unbeliever, but not if it requires your own private interpretation to be understood. The blind man whom Jesus healed had a powerful testimony: "One thing I do know, that, whereas I was blind, now I see" (John 9:25). It was a personal experience. But it was also one that anybody, believer or unbeliever, could examine in an objective, logical, honest manner. Anyone could find out that the man had indeed been blind and in fact could now see. His experience was not a private, subjective one, but one that could be examined. The same is true of Frank and Charlie. Their testimony was not some private, mystical happenstance; rather, as Lou himself observed, "Those two used to be the most obnoxious #&$%¢*'s I've ever met. But now they are the most humble loving men I could ever imagine."

WHAT ABOUT LOU?

At the time of this writing, Lou has not yet received Jesus Christ as his own God and Savior — but Greg tells me he is getting closer every day.

NOTES

1. Carl Jung, quoted in *Bits and Pieces,* May 1978, p. 18.

8 • Why Do the Innocent Suffer?

Dan first met Jack at the bowl of avocado dip after one of our Bible discussion parties. Within a few minutes he had learned three things about Jack: he was a medical doctor, he loved avocado dip, and he hated God.

"How did you like the discussion?" Dan inquired.

"Super," Jack mumbled, stuffing an avocado-smothered chip into his mouth. "But let me tell you something. If there is a God, I don't want anything to do with Him."

"Really? How come?"

"Because He made a world full of suffering. People around me hurt from diseases they didn't do anything to get. I see babies born with deformities and children neglected until they get sick or die. If God is so all-powerful and so all-fired good and loving, why did He create this mess, and why doesn't He do something about it?"

"Well," Dan said, "first, let's consider the obvious. Much, if not most, of the suffering in the world is directly caused by people who inflict it on themselves or on others — not by an act of God."

"Sure," Jack agreed, though his eyes expressed an inward dissatisfaction with Dan's answer. "People cause suffering! But that's only part of it. What about the disease and birth defects they don't cause? And what about natural disasters? And —"

"Wait a minute," Dan interrupted. "Let's take one thing at a time."

"All right," Jack agreed. "Let's start with this one — why doesn't God just wipe out all suffering right now?"

"If He did," Dan answered, "He would also have to wipe out the cause of all suffering. And since all people cause some suffering, we would all have to be wiped out."

The guests trying to reach around them made it a bit embarrassing to monopolize the avocado dip any longer, so Dan and Jack made their way to the punch bowl as they talked.

"Why not just make us so we couldn't cause suffering?" Jack demanded. He poured himself a glass of what looked to Dan like orange sherbet floating in pink lemonade. Then, gesturing with the ladle, he made an offer to pour Dan some. Dan reluctantly held out a glass as he answered.

"You mean like a robot or a computer? You see, in order to keep us from being a source of suffering, God would have to remove our ability to choose. Then we would just be a machine that God manipulated."

"What's wrong with that?" Jack countered.

"Well, if we could not choose, we would not be able to love. The only way we can have a love relationship with someone is if that someone has a free choice not to love us. A computer cannot love because it cannot choose. We could get it to print out 'I love you' if we program it to say 'I love you,' but that's not love. Love requires choice."

Dan sketched this on a napkin:

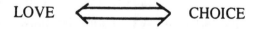

LOVE ⟸⟹ CHOICE

"But," Jack persisted, "what about suffering from nature? At least God could remove things like death, sickness, and tragedies."

"The Bible says those things exist because the natural universe (including man) is cursed. God created it perfect — a Garden of Eden. But when Adam disobeyed, he took mankind down a path of suffering. If you choose to walk on a path that includes suffering, then, of course, you suffer the things on that path. The disease and the disasters of nature are a physical reflection of man's spiritual choice to take the path away from God."

"Why not just give Adam a place to live away from God?" Jack continued. "Why make the whole earth a place of suffering?"

"Well," Dan answered, "the Bible says, 'The secret things belong to the LORD our God, but the things revealed belong to us and to our sons forever, that we may observe all the words of this law' [Deuteronomy 29:29]. So I might not be able to tell you why God did what He did, but I can tell you why what He did seems reasonable."

"OK, shoot!"

The flow of bodies around the dining room table gradually backed them up to a leaning position against a wall. Dan nursed his sherbet-soaked lemonade as he answered.

"All choices have results. If the result of one choice isn't any different from the result of another choice, then the choice has no significance. If you come to a fork in the road, you have an opportunity to decide which path to take. Your choice to go a certain way is significant only if there really is a road that goes that way. I can't choose to take the dirt path that leads to the swimming hole if there is no dirt path that leads to the swimming hole. On the other hand, if there really is such a path, and I choose to take it to the swimming hole, then I will indeed have to walk on that path.

"Adam chose the path of disobedience and 'death,' which actually contained all the suffering we now observe. After heading down that path awhile, Adam and Eve had children who, of course, were born on that path of suffering. Then their children had children and so on until finally you and I were also born on that path of suffering.

"Now the point here is that in order for the choice Adam made to be significant, the result we now have (a suffering universe) must be real. If there was no result, no suffering, on the road of disobedience that Adam chose, then his choice would not have been significant. Choice and its results are inseparable."

Dan sketched this on a different napkin:

$$\text{CHOICE} \Longleftrightarrow \text{RESULTS}$$

When they had moved from the punch bowl to the wall, Dan had stuffed the first napkin in his pocket. Now he got it out and put the two together.

$$\text{LOVE} \Longleftrightarrow \text{CHOICE} \Longleftrightarrow \text{RESULTS}$$

"Remember, Jack," he continued, "we already agreed that love and choice are inseparable. Since choice requires results, love and results are also inseparable. If God is loving, it would seem He would give Adam a choice to love Him or not. That would mean that the result of that choice must really be there."

"But why make the result so severe?" Jack asked.

"Well, the greater the love, the greater the choice, and the greater the result," Dan continued. "As we look back on thousands of years of suffering, we can see that the result of Adam's choice — contrasted with the Garden of Eden — was very great. So we now know that choice was also very great, and therefore the love God gave us the capacity to have is very great.''

When Jack and Dan looked around, they discovered that most of the people had already left. They decided to go home and let the host and hostess go to bed. The next week they had another meeting of the Bible discussion group. Jack had an emergency case that made him miss the meeting, but he came afterward to talk more about suffering — and eat.

"I've been thinking over what you said," Jack began, as he generously piled a plate with sandwiches, brownies, cheese balls, potato chips, and a big gob of avocado dip. "And I've got some more questions. Why couldn't God put off the result of Adam's sin? That way we wouldn't have to suffer."

"But," Dan answered, "if God put off the result of the first sin, then He'd have to put off the result of the second sin, and then the third, and so on — including yours and mine. If He kept on putting it off, then there would be no result. Then no choice, nor love, would be possible. If, on the other hand, God allowed the result at any time, then the suffering we now observe would follow."

"Well, then," Jack pleaded, "why did He create us at all? I mean, I never asked to be here, yet here I am in the midst of a world of suffering."

"Of course, God could have not bothered to create a being like man. He could have been satisfied with things that could not choose. But remember, that would mean He was satisfied to not see love in His creation. If He's going to have love in His creation, He has to allow choice, which means that rejection and its result must be available."

"Couldn't God just make everybody perfect and make the universe a place without suffering?"

"Well —"

"Wait! Let me guess," Jack interrupted as he answered his own question. "If He made us perfect, without our having anything to say about it, we would just be perfect robots without choice. Then we would not be able to love. Right?"

"Right!"

"But wait a minute," Jack continued. "Since we are born on this imperfect path of suffering, why couldn't God set before us a clear choice of perfection, and let us choose whether we wanted to stay on this suffering road or not? Then everybody who wanted it could be made perfect, get off this path, and have no suffering."

"Excellent idea," Dan marveled. "I think God would wholeheartedly agree!"

"You do? What makes you think so?"

"Because that's exactly what He did!"

"He did?"

"Yes. God the Son invaded this planet as the man Jesus Christ and provided that example of perfection. All the people who want Him are free to receive Him as their own God and Savior. The result of that choice is that we will be guided through this present, cursed, suffering world into an eternity of non-suffering."

"You mean heaven?" Jack asked.

"Yes. God told Adam that if he chose to disobey Him, it would result in death. Looking back on thousands of years of history, we see that 'death' meant a lot of suffering. In the same way, God is telling us to obey Him and 'choose *life* in order that you may live' [Deuteronomy 30:19]. That life includes an eternal future where 'He shall wipe away every tear from their eyes; and there shall no longer be any death; there shall no longer be any mourning, or crying, or pain; the first things have passed away' [Revelation 21:4]."

WHY SUFFERING?

Let us summarize. Jack asked nine major questions about why a fair, loving God would allow suffering. Here is a recap of those questions with a brief statement of the answer given for each:

1. WHY IS THE WORLD FULL OF SUFFERING?

There are lots of reasons for suffering, but man himself is a major cause. People cause most of the agony we observe. In America the divorce rate continues to climb, the suicide and homicide rates are increasing, and the general crime rate is up in most areas. All that causes suffering, and it is all man-made.

2. WHY DOESN'T GOD WIPE OUT ALL SUFFERING RIGHT NOW?

In order for God to wipe out all suffering, He would also have to wipe out the cause of all suffering. Since all people cause some suffering, that solution would require that all people be wiped out.

3. WHY DOESN'T GOD MAKE PEOPLE UNABLE TO CAUSE SUF-FERING?

To do that, God would have to make people unable to choose. But love requires choice. That solution would make a love relationship with God — or one another — impossible. A husband, wife, or friend can love you only if he or she has a completely free option to *not* love you. If the other person cannot choose *not* to love you, then real love is impossible.

4. WHY DOES GOD MAKE US SUFFER THINGS LIKE DISEASE AND NATURAL DISASTERS?

Nature was originally created without suffering — a Garden of Eden. It was lowered to its present perverted state (Romans 8:20-22) to match the spiritually perverted state man placed himself in through sin. It is not that God makes us suffer. God provided us with the option of rejecting Him, and the consequences consistent with that choice included the perversion of nature.

5. WHY DID GOD MAKE THE RESULTS OF ADAM'S CHOICE SO BAD?

Without results, choice is insignificant. Suppose I offer you one of two milk chocolate candy bars — a Hershey bar or a Nestles bar. If the result of eating one is the same as the result of eating the other, then the result of choosing one is the same as the result of choosing the other. In that case, the choice would be insignificant. Now let us imagine a situation in which the result of your eating would be very different. Suppose one item offered was a milk chocolate bar and the other a chocolate-flavored laxative. Then the choice would be significant because the results of eating the two would be very different.

If God is going to give man the real choice of following Him or not, then the results of the choice must also be real.

6. WHY ARE WE SUFFERING BECAUSE OF ADAM'S SIN?

In order for us *not* to suffer because of Adam's sin, God would have to remove the results of that sin. If God removed the result of Adam's sin, then He would have to keep doing that for everybody's sin, including yours and mine, to keep suffering from starting. But if God kept removing the result of our choosing to sin, then of course there would be no result at all — and, as reasoned above, no choice or love would be possible.

7. WHY DID GOD MAKE US, ANYWAY?

Again, we cannot say why God did what He did; but what He did seems reasonable. Because God is the ultimate good, anything He does to display Himself is a good thing to do. (The only reason it is bad for man to display himself is because he is full of badness.) Part of God's goodness is that He is loving. As we described above, love requires choice.

So if God is good, to display His love in His creation He must create someone who can choose. Without a being like man who could choose, there would be no loving relationship within God's creation.

8. WHY DOESN'T GOD JUST MAKE EVERYBODY PERFECT AND THE UNIVERSE A PLACE WITHOUT SUFFERING?

The answer to "Why doesn't God make everyone perfect and the universe without suffering?" is, of course, the same as for the previous question. If God made us perfect without our choosing to be perfect, we would be robots without the ability to love.

That brings us logically to the final question:

9. WHY DOESN'T GOD LET US CHOOSE TO GET OUT OF THIS SUFFERING NOW?

The answer to "Why doesn't God let us choose to get out of this suffering?" is that He does. That is what the gospel says. God is begging us to choose Him by receiving Jesus Christ. The result of that decision will be an eternal life of nonsuffering that will be infinitely superior to the temporal pain we now know.

A Believer's Perspective

Basically, we have given two reasons for suffering: things people do to others or themselves and the cursed nature in which we live. In addition to those, there are many reasons why *Christians* suffer. A Christian may be under God's discipline or direction. We may be convicted of our own sin. We also suffer simply because we belong to Christ and are not part of this world system. The one who knows the power of sin is not the one who is living in sin, but the one who is attempting to be righteous. "If you think it's weak to be meek," it's been said, "try being meek for a week."

If you are riding a raft downstream, you never feel the

strength of the current. Only when you get off and try to walk back against it do you realize its power. Walking against the flow of the stream causes suffering by the very nature of the fact that the stream is going the other way. So it is with a Christian living for God in a world system that pushes like a current in the opposite direction.

But all these valid causes of *Christian* suffering are inappropriate answers to give the nonbeliever struggling with the question. The fact is, the flow of this life contains some elements of suffering that will be there no matter which way you are going. They are part of the very nature of the stream. It is those things that are within the realm of the unbeliever's life experience, and those are the issues we have dealt with here.

WHAT ABOUT JACK?

Jack and Dan met together several times. One night after a discussion Jack stayed late. They talked until about 1:00 A.M. Jack realized his need for Jesus Christ and prayed with Dan, receiving Him as his personal God and Savior.

9 • Can Good Deeds Get Us to Heaven?

Strips of sunlight pierced the overhanging branches and glanced off the water. "What a perfect morning for fishing," Phil thought. The glassy stillness of the lake was disturbed only by occasional ripples set in motion by the gentle rocking of the boat.

Actually, the beauty of the east Tennessee sunrise had only interrupted his thoughts, which quickly returned to Ray, the man sitting behind him in the boat. Phil figured that Ray's call asking him to go fishing was an answer to prayer for an "open door." They had been friends for a long time, but Phil's attempts to convey his faith in Jesus Christ to Ray had been fruitless. Ray would always say something like, "My faith is a personal thing, and I really don't like to talk about it," thus slamming the door shut on the conversation. Beside that, Phil began to feel he was getting a reputation with Ray as a religious "weirdo." He resorted to prayer — prayer that God would make Ray curious. When he called, Phil sensed that an answer was on the way.

They had settled into serious fishing. Neither talked for several minutes at a time. After a while, Ray said, "You know what those people in my wife's church believe?"

"No. What?"

"They think you don't have to do anything good to be a Christian."

"Really?"

Five minutes of quiet fishing passed.

"What do *you* think?" Ray asked suddenly.

"What do I think about what?" Phil's calm voice hid his excitement at seeing God create spiritual interest in his non-Christian friend.

"About what those people in my wife's church think," Ray returned with mounting exasperation.

"Oh, that." Phil thought a few seconds before he mischievously said, "Well, if I talked about that, I'd be discussing my personal beliefs, and I don't like to talk about my *personal* beliefs."

This time about twenty minutes of quiet fishing went by. Then Ray interrupted the silence again.

"Well, if you *were* going to talk about it, what would you say?"

"What would I say about what, Ray?"

"The idea that you don't have to be good to get to heaven!"

Phil responded casually, "I guess I'd just say what the Bible says."

"Well, what does it say?"

"Acutally," Phil answered, "the Bible says you have to be perfect to go to heaven."

"Perfect!"

"Yep. Jesus took the two most outwardly righteous groups of His day as an example and said, 'For I say to you, that unless your righteousness surpasses that of the scribes and the Pharisees, you shall not enter the kingdom of heaven' [Matthew 5:20]. A little later He went on to say, 'You are to be perfect, as your heavenly Father is perfect' [Matthew 5:48]. Heaven, then, is a place where there is *no* sin, not just a place where there is *not much* sin or a place where people live who have tried real hard not to be sinful. God will only allow perfect people in heaven. Now Ray, if you were going to get a new window in your house, you wouldn't want one that had a big old crack in it, even though there were some pieces that were OK. An unbroken window is not just a window with some unbroken pieces in it. In the same way, heaven is not a place for pretty good people with only some sin.''

"That sounds just the opposite from what my wife's church believes.''

"What they probably mean,'' Phil continued, "is that Jesus Christ paid for all our sins. The Bible says when Jesus died on the cross, He 'perfected for all time those who are sanctified' [Hebrews 10:14].''

"What does it mean to be sanctified?'' Ray wanted to know.

"It means to be made holy,'' Phil answered. "And we become holy when we accept God's gift of forgiveness by receiving Christ into our life. Christ paid for all sins of all time. So when we receive Him, God doesn't see any of our sin anymore.''

"But then why not become a Christian and live as bad as you can?'' Ray asked.

"Because when a person receives Christ, he is born into God's family. When that happens, the Holy Spirit comes into a person and changes his desires. Lots of people act like Christianity is just a human religion, so they invent lots of rules to keep people in line. Actually, since it's really of God, the Spirit of God within the believer convicts him of sin and teaches him godliness from inside out as he studies the Bible and fellowships with other believers. After you are born into a certain family, you can rebel against everything your parents tell you, but the natural thing in a good family is a desire to please your parents. When you receive Christ, you not only have a new birth but a new daddy — God!''

HOW DO I GET TO BE GOOD?

How good do you have to be to get to heaven? How good is good enough? And why not become a believer, yet live as bad as you can? Human beings from Socrates to Ghandi have struggled with those questions, but only the Bible has a solution. As we encounter people with questions in this area, we need to keep several facts in mind. The questions that usually come up are:

1. HOW GOOD DOES GOD WANT ME TO BE?

God requires perfection. He told Abraham that he needed to be "blameless" (Genesis 17:1). God told Moses to tell Israel, "You shall be holy, for I the Lord your God am holy" (Leviticus 19:2). Jesus said, "You are to be perfect, as your heavenly Father is perfect." (Matthew 5:48). The context of Jesus' words is the importance of righteousness (verses 20-28). Later on, the apostle Peter reminded the early church that God said, "YOU SHALL BE HOLY, FOR I AM HOLY" (1 Peter 1:16).

God's standard never falls short of complete righteousness and holiness. Anything less than perfection is sin. Sin causes suffering. Because heaven is a place of no suffering, it must also be a place of no sin, not just a place of not much sin or a place for people who tried hard not to sin. If suffering is to be done away with, sin must be eliminated, not just minimized. If we suppose God will accept the better people of this world, those with the least amount of sin, we are still asking God to accept sin. As Phil illustrated it to Ray, an unbroken window is not simply one with some unbroken spots in it.

Those who believe God should accept them because they are relatively good have not taken a close look at themselves. Social psychologist Jerald Jellison estimates that the average

American outstrips Pinocchio by telling 200 lies a *day*.[1] That is 73,000 lies a year! How old are you? If you are thirty, that's 2,190,000 sins you would have to explain away. If you are forty, it is nearly 3 million — and that is only lies. Now do the same for gossip, jealousy, outbursts of anger, disputes, dissensions, factions and so on — see Galatians 5:19-21 for a start. No one comes even close to being righteous.

2. HOW DO I GET TO BE GOOD?

The second crucial factor in this issue is that God made perfection available as a free gift. By dying on the cross, Jesus Christ "perfected for all time those who are sanctified" (Hebrews 10:14). You see, God "made Him who knew no sin to be sin on our behalf, that we might become the righteousness of God in Him" (2 Corinthians 5:21) We swap our sins for Christ's perfection. At that specific time in history, "God was in Christ reconciling the world to Himself, not counting their trespasses against them" (2 Corinthians 5:19). So whether we are Hitler or Ghandi, our sins are *no longer the issue* in beginning our relationship with God. The only issue involved is what we do about Jesus Christ.

If a criminal is handed a pardon, the issue is no longer his crime but rather what he will do about the pardon. If he refuses it, he will remain in prison. The questions, Why is he in prison? and, Why is he not out of prison? have two different answers. He is *in* prison because he is a convicted criminal. He is *not out of* prison because he refused the pardon. In the same way, the answer to the question, Why will a person be in hell? is, Because he is a sinner, but the answer to the question, Why will he not be in heaven? is, because he did not receive Christ.

Many unbelievers, concerned about how relatively good or bad they are, need to realize that their sins no longer have anything whatsoever to do with beginning a relationship with

God. All those sins have already been paid for. That is what the Bible means when it says we are being offered salvation on the basis of "grace" (unmerited favor, Ephesians 2:8-9), and "mercy" (unmerited noncondemnation, Titus 3:5). Mankind is being offered a pardon. That pardon, Jesus Christ, is the only issue before us.

3. WHY NOT BECOME A CHRISTIAN AND LIVE AS BAD AS YOU CAN?

If Christianity were only a religion made up by people, the question "Why not become a Christian and then live as bad as you can?" would be a legitimate concern. Expecting people to get better just because they prayed a prayer makes no more sense than pardoning all convicts and expecting them to become model citizens. We would certainly ask, "How do we know they won't just accept the pardon and live as bad as they can?"

But with salvation there is one big difference: it is from God, not man. When we receive Christ, God comes into us and changes us from the inside out. The Bible says, "Therefore if any man is in Christ, he is a new creature; the old things passed away; behold, new things have come" (2 Corinthians 5:17).

Then, too, there is the fact that receiving Christ makes you part of God's family, and God takes care of His family. The author of Hebrews says, "God deals with you as with sons; for what son is there whom his father does not discipline?" (Hebrews 12:7). Also, being in a good family generally motivates people to be part of what that family stands for. So it is with the family of God.

WHAT ABOUT RAY?

Ray accepted Jesus Christ as his personal God and Savior some time after the fishing trip. Phil's sensitivity to God's leading here contains some exciting lessons for us.

For one thing, Phil was able to turn the situation over to God while remaining available for God to use him. Paul exhorted the Colossians, "Devote yourselves to prayer, keeping alert in it with an attitude of thanksgiving; praying at the same time for us as well, that God may open up to us a door for the word, so that we may speak forth the mystery of Christ, for which I have also been imprisoned" (Colossians 4:2-3). The key to friendship evangelism is to use both prayer and friendship.

Another principle is observed in the fact that Phil motivated Ray through his conversation. When he realized he was beginning to sound like a "religious weirdo," Phil backed off and let God do the initiating. And when He did, Phil gave only short incomplete answers until Ray was ready to hear the whole gospel. We must motivate our hearers to keep asking questions.

In the passage just mentioned, Paul went on to say, "Let your speech always be with grace, seasoned, as it were, with salt, so that you may know how you should respond to each person" (Colossians 4:6). I can still hear Professor Howard Hendricks of Dallas Theological Seminary saying "You can lead a horse to water, but you can't make him drink — but you *can* feed him salt!" Does our conversation with unbelievers leave them thirsty to hear more about God?

NOTES

1. Hedley Donovan, ed., "Ground Rules for Telling Lies," *Time,* 3 April 1978, p. 67.

10 • How About the Hypocrites?

Winter brings an avalanche of people to the ski country of Aspen, Colorado. If we were there, our senses would be captivated by the crisp air, the softness of fresh snow under-foot, and the intriguing snowcapped peaks that surround that area. Possibly, though, we would be just as intrigued and just as captivated by the conversations that take place in the lodges, cabins, and cafes of that unique little town.

In one such cafe after one such day of skiing sat four people, two couples who came to Aspen with a group from Fort Worth. They finished their meal and the two wives engaged in a conversation with each other. The men sat quietly awhile. Then Mac broke the silence.

"I've been thinking," he said, "and I've come to the sad conclusion that I don't want my daughters to live like anyone I know." He then sat quietly a few more seconds, sipping his hot chocolate, his eyes gazing at the still but steady snowfall outside the cafe window. Then, coming out of his trance, he looked at John and continued, "What's even sadder, I don't want them to live like I do either!"

John nodded an understanding response. He was not sure what to say. Mac had been his friend since high school. As a lawyer, John had represented him; as a real estate investor, Mac rented John his office space. But there was one thing they did not share — John's faith in the Lord Jesus Christ.

John had been a Christian for years, but Mac thought his beliefs were all foolishness. Five years before that Aspen conversation, John had tried to make a case for Christianity by showing it was responsible for all the social progress and moral improvements of the human race. Mac had said, "Aw, that's your idea. I think the Irish potato did all of that!" It was the end of their conversation about Christianity for five years. But John had kept praying for God to give him an opportunity, a second chance. This looked like it. They both had teenagers and were naturally concerned about their future.

"I know what you mean," John finally answered. "I don't want mine to live like I do either."

"Really?" Mac seemed surprised. "Then how would you like them to live?"

"Like Jesus of Nazareth," John answered.

"Oh, good grief!" Mac returned. "Not me. Christianity is full of hypocrites, and I sure don't want my daughters to be like that."

"I didn't say anything about Christianity," John continued. "I'm sure Christianity is as full of hypocrites as anything else that's valuable. Light always tends to attract bugs, you know. Any good idea will attract people who want to get in on a good thing without really being part of it. What I meant was, I want my teenagers to live like Jesus Christ."

"But if Jesus had the true religion, why do so many of the people who believe in Him turn into hypocrites?" Mac asked.

"The Bible doesn't say that everyone who believes in Jesus Christ will be perfect, just perfectly forgiven. Actually, a biblical Christian is one who admits that he is a sinner, which is just the opposite of a hypocrite. A hypocrite is someone who outwardly pretends to be good."

"But," Mac objected, "if believing in Jesus is going to be

worthwhile, it seems like He ought to make people better morally.''

"Are you sure He doesn't?" John answered, finishing off his hot chocolate. He continued, "You see, if somebody receives Christ into his life, the Spirit of God begins to work on his desires so that after a while he should be changing for the better."

"I know some real creepy people that are supposed to be Christians," Mac broke in.

"Sure," John continued, "but you need to compare them with what they were, not with what they would be if they were instantly perfect. The inconsistencies in their life should be steadily decreasing, but that doesn't mean they've arrived. If a guy five feet tall who weighed 250 pounds spoke to us about great eating habits, we'd probably call him a hypocrite. But if we learned he weighed 300 pounds a month ago, that would change the picture."

"Well," Mac insisted, "it still seems to me that if the Bible is right, we should be able to look at people who associate themselves with it and see better people."

"Any product must be considered by looking at that product itself," John reasoned. "You wouldn't recommend that people quit working for a company because some other people just work there to make money."

"I don't know," Mac exclaimed. "I guess there's just something in me that hates hypocrites!"

"Well, you're in good company," John said. "You and I and Jesus all agree about that. As a matter of fact, when Jesus was talking to some religious hypocrites, He said, 'You serpents, you brood of vipers, how shall you escape the sentence of hell?' [Matthew 23:33]."

"I sure wouldn't want to be a hypocrite," Mac added. "That's why I'm not a Christian, I guess."

"But Mac," John insisted, "the very fact that you don't think you're good enough to be a pattern for your daughters makes you the opposite of a hypocrite. A hypocrite is somebody who outwardly pretends he is something he's not. A hypocrite would never admit he can't be perfect."

WHAT ABOUT HYPOCRITES?

Mac and John discussed five crucial aspects of this issue. Let us look at them a little more closely. They were:

1. WHY ARE THERE SO MANY HYPOCRITES IN CHRISTIANITY?

If Christianity is to be doubted because there are hypocrites in our churches, we must first be sure those hypocrites are really Christians. The legitimacy of anything original cannot be judged by qualities of a phony.

My grandmother used to send away for the best recipes. But when they came, she would substitute ingredients she already had on hand for those listed in the recipe. Lard was substituted for butter, regular salt for seasoned salt, and so on. When the dish came out tasting sort of funny and nobody ate much, she would write to the company and tell them what she thought of their recipe.

Unregenerate people who go through Christian-sounding religious formalities without having received Jesus Christ as their God and Savior are not real Christians. The presence of such hypocrites is just a fact of life about anything worthwhile. There are false diamonds in jewelry because real diamonds are valuable. We make copies of Rembrandt's paintings because the real ones are priceless. Quacks spring up in the medical profession because good doctors are an asset to the community. Actually, the fact that Christianity attracts phonies is a good indication that it is real. As John recognized, "Light always tends to attract bugs."

2. IF JESUS HAD THE TRUE RELIGION, WHY DOESN'T HE KEEP HIS FOLLOWERS FROM TURNING INTO HYPOCRITES?

There is no claim in the Bible that true believers in Jesus Christ become perfect in this life. A true believer is one who recognizes his sinfulness and need for Jesus Christ as his Savior. (see 1 John 1:8-10). Although Christians do change for the better, the change is from the inside out. It does not begin with outward appearances, as it does with hypocrites.

Jesus was harder on the hypocrites than on any other group. His words in Matthew 23 are considered by many to be the harshest language He ever used. Jesus was talking to and about hypocrites. It is interesting to contrast our Lord's description of a hypocrite in Matthew 23 with the Bible's description of a real believer.

Hypocrites, Jesus said, "do all their deeds to be noticed by men" (v. 5), whereas biblical believers seek only to be approved by God (Romans 6:5-6, Colossians 3:23; Ephesians 5:10).

Hypocrisy turns people off from religion (verse 13), but godliness reasons with people in a gentle, understanding way (Acts 28:23-24; 1 Thessalonians 2:7-8).

Hypocrites train others to be what they are. Speaking about their converts, Jesus told them, "You make him twice as much a son of hell as yourselves" (v. 15). But real Christians train others to be like Christ, not like themselves (Matthew 28:18-20).

Hypocrites deal with external formalism, neglecting internal qualities (vv. 25-27). Biblical believers, on the other hand, emphasize inner attitudes, knowing that God changes people from within (Galatians 5:22-24).

3. IF JESUS REALLY CHANGES PEOPLE, WHY AREN'T ALL CHRISTIANS MORALLY BETTER THAN ALL NON-CHRISTIANS?

Though God does deal with true believers, He does not

make them perfect all at once. It is a great compliment to Christianity that people expect Christians to be better people. But some people expect instantaneous change. When someone complains to me that a certain person who claims to have received Christ is living inconsistently, I generally respond with something like, "Maybe so. But if you really want to know whether there's anything to his faith or not, look at him closely. Get to know him really well. See if there *has* been any change in his life. But be careful," I warn, "you might find Christ that way, and when you receive Him but are not yet perfect, other may think *you're* a hypocrite."

Even Christians forget how long it takes to grow. Frequently people tell me how disappointed they are in old So-and-So, who received Christ two weeks ago and has not yet joined the church or attended their Bible study. Besides that, he still smokes and goes to the tavern. I assure them that, over a period of time, changes should be noticeable. But I also ask them, "If I made a list of all *your* actions and attitudes two weeks ago and another list today, how much change would I notice? Probably not much! But that does not mean you are not really a Christian or the Spirit of God is not working in your life. It is just that God works from the inside, and real growth takes time. It is hypocrisy that emphasizes overnight change in external appearances."

4. IF SOME CHRISTIANS ARE HYPOCRITES, DOESN'T THAT SUGGEST THAT CHRISTIANITY HAS SOME MISTAKES IN IT?

We must encourage people to consider Jesus Christ and the Bible, rather than what people do with them. Any product must be evaluated on its own grounds. We do not stop going to hospitals because some doctors are in medicine just for the prestige and wealth they can accumulate. Either hospitals are a good idea or they are not. If they are, then insincere doctors do not make them a bad idea.

Jesus must be presented to people as God, and the Bible must be presented as God's verbal revelation to man. That often requires getting our hearers off the hypocritical things that have been done with Jesus Christ or the Scripture and getting them back to the real product itself.

5. HOW CAN I BECOME A CHRISTIAN IF I HATE ITS HYPOCRISY?

To hate hypocrisy is to agree with Jesus. It is helpful for someone to realize that you and he and Jesus Christ are all on the same side of this issue. You might further point out Christ's own comment that hypocrites would not "escape the sentence of hell" (Matthew 23:33). So, if a certain unbeliever dislikes hypocrites, that is good. But you might help him question the wisdom of his decision to spend eternity with them. To not receive Christ is to end up the same as the hypocrites — eternally speaking.

WHAT ABOUT MAC?

After the conversation in Aspen, Mac asked John where his teenage daughters could go to get more information about the Bible. John steered them to a neighborhood teenage group where, after a while, both girls received Jesus Christ as their personal Savior. One day at lunch, about a year later, Mac said to John, "You know, this Christianity has not exactly created peace and tranquility in our home. My daughters are telling me I'm not a Christian, and you know, I think they are right." A little bit later, Mac received Jesus Christ as his personal Savior — following in his daughters' footsteps.

11 • What Does It Mean to Believe?

Sue was a regular Mrs. Clean, as "together" as her house was. She had the latest clothes and the best hairstyle, and she radiated Southern hospitality — she wasn't even overweight!

As Betty drove up to Sue's house, her thoughts raced back to last Saturday's party where they first met. Betty had looked forward to the get-acquainted party as a possible escape from her typical Christian routine. Not that she had any great problem — but then maybe that was the problem. Her husband and family were Christians and so were her friends, *all* her friends. She wanted to be effective for God to those unbelievers around her. The problem was, she had not even gotten to *know* any unbelievers around her, much less ever led anyone to Christ.

Probably out of sheer desperation she forced an introduction of herself on Sue at the party. When Sue invited her (along with her two preschoolers) to lunch, she was so elated that she forgot her usual uneasiness about talking to new people. But now, standing in front of Sue's immaculate and obviously expensive house, a short bundle of energy tugging at each arm, all Betty's hesitations returned. And it was not just because Betty wanted to win a soul to Christ. She had really begun to like Sue and was genuinely concerned about her.

But how could Betty ever find a way to talk with Sue about

God? She did not appear to have any need for Him. There seemed to be no way.

During lunch, groping for something to talk about, Betty asked, "Do ya'll go to church?"

"Well — we don't go very much," Sue answered, half shouting from the kitchen, where she had gone to get the coffeepot. "My husband doesn't like it much, so we generally just go on Christmas and Easter. Now that the kids are old enough for Sunday school, I think we will start going again." Her voice quieted down as she returned to the dining room.

"Why do you want your children to go?"

"Oh, I've always believed in God," Sue explained. "And, well, I just think their education would be lacking if they didn't learn about Christianity."

"Would you mind telling me how you'd describe your relationship with God?" Betty inquired. At that, Sue went into her background of attending a mainline denominational church as a child, then getting away from it when she went to college.

"Would you say you've ever come to the place where you know for sure you'd go to heaven if you died?" Betty asked.

"Not really."

"Did you know that the Bible says you can know that?"

"No. Does it?"

"Uh-huh. If you have a Bible, I'll show you."

Sue left and came back with what appeared to be an old family Bible that Aunt Somebody-or-Other must have given her way back when. It looked like it had never been opened past the cover page. Betty turned to 1 John 5, then gave it back to Sue. Pointing to verse thirteen, Betty asked, "Would you read this, and tell me what you think it means?"

" 'These things have I written unto you who believe on the

name of the Son of God, that ye may know that ye have eternal life (KJV*)' — But that says you have to believe," Sue argued. "What if I don't believe enough for it to take?"

"What do you mean by 'believe enough'?" Betty asked.

"I mean, I have too many doubts," Sue continued. "I'd like to believe in God and Jesus completely, but to be honest with you, I have lots of trouble doing that."

"I think the Bible has a different definition of faith than what you're thinking about," Betty said. "It doesn't just mean lack of doubt. Let me show you another verse." Taking the big black Bible off Sue's lap, Betty thumbed over to the gospel of John, chapter one, and read verse twelve. " 'But as many as received him, to them gave He power to become the sons of God, even to them that believe on his name (KJV).' You see, believing is a decision to receive Jesus Christ into your life as your own God and Savior, not some feeling that you don't have any doubts."

"But how much faith do you need to have to receive Christ?" Sue asked.

"It's not an amount," Betty answered, "it's a choice. You see, Sue, the Bible says that you get to God by faith, not works."

"Oh, yes. I remember being taught that in Sunday school."

"But," Betty continued, "if faith was some degree of believing you had to conjure up, some amount of 'nondoubt' you had to achieve, it would be a work."

"You mean it's enough to just say I believe in Jesus?"

"No. You need to receive Him."

"Well, what's the difference?"

---

*King James Version.

About that time, the dining room was invaded by Betty's four-year-old with Sue's three-year-old in hot pursuit. That sort of interruption had been common, and Betty was tempted to quit and go home several times. But she felt Sue was close to making a decision, so she pressed on.

"May I borrow a pen?" Betty asked. Sue reached over and handed her the pen that had been sitting next to her on the table.

"Let's suppose you needed a pen for something, and I said I would give you this one." Betty held out the pen as she continued talking. "Do you believe I'd give you this pen?"

"Yes, I guess so," Sue answered.

"Then why don't you have it?"

"Well — because — because you haven't given it to me."

"I've made it available. I've offered it to you," Betty went on, "and you said you'd believe me if I said I'd give it to you."

"Yes —"

"But we could sit here all day, and you could believe that way and never get the pen. Lots of people believe about Jesus the way you believe about the pen, but since they've never received Him, they don't have Him any more than you have the pen. What *would* you have to do to get the pen?"

"I'd have to take it, I guess," Sue realized.

"Well, go ahead," Betty coaxed. But Sue hesitated. Just then one of her children, who had been watching the offer, reached up and grabbed the pen. "Well!" Betty exclaimed. "If that was God's offer of eternal life through Christ, your daughter would have it, but you would still be without it — faith and all."

They both laughed a little, then Betty continued, "Sue, I'd like to invite you to receive Christ as your personal God and

Savior right now. Is there anything keeping you from doing that?''

"I think I've already done that," Sue answered. "I went forward in my church when I was little."

"Now Sue," Betty reasoned, "you konw as well as I if you grew up in a conservative church and did *not* go forward sometime or other, you'd be the exception instead of the rule. Tell me, what did you say to God when you went forward, what decision did you make?"

"I don't remember saying anything." Sue chuckled. "Everybody in my Sunday school class went forward. I was the last holdout, and my teacher wanted a perfect record."

"I don't know if you received Christ then or not," Betty went on. "But since you weren't sure that you'd go to heaven, why don't you pray again with me right now."

"But I pray every day."

"Have you prayed for God to forgive all your sins?" Betty inquired.

"I ask Him to forgive my sins every night."

"Then you may have never asked Him into your life to cleanse you."

"Why do you say that?" Sue asked.

"Because then you never have to ask for that again."

"Well, I do think I should begin studying the Bible more," Sue concluded. "For me, this will be a long process of study."

"That's great," Betty answered. "But the first step in understanding the Bible is to have the Spirit of God inside you, making it clear to you. I'd be glad to meet with you regularly, if you'd like."

"That would be great," Sue answered.

"Of course, we must do it God's way. All right?" Betty insisted.

"Sure."

"But God's way is for you to begin by receiving Jesus Christ as your own God and Savior. Would you make sure of that with a prayer right now?"

Sue agreed. She prayed: "Dear God, I realize that I'm a sinner and that Jesus Christ paid for my sins on the cross. I invite Jesus into my life as my God and Savior right now. Thanks. Amen."

BELIEVING IS RECEIVING

The initial believing that introduces someone into God's family is expressed in the Bible by a key word: *receive*. When writing to the Corinthians, Paul said, "The gospel which I preached to you, which also you *received* . . . I also *received*" (1 Corinthians 15:1, 3, italics added). When reasoning with the Colossian believers, he said, "You therefore have *received* Christ Jesus" (2:6, italics added). He explained to the Thessalonians about "those who perish, because they did not *receive* the love of the truth so as to be saved" (2 Thessalonians 2:10, italics added). In his letter to the Galatians, Paul wrote concerning the "gospel" that they *"received"* (1:9, italics added). It is the apostle John, however, who seems to have expressed it the most clearly when he defined "those who believe in His name" as those who *"received* Him" (John 1:12, italics added).

With patience, but also persistence, Betty used five questions to lead Sue to an understanding that she needed to *receive* Christ. After talking with many people who frequently lead others to Christ (one per week or more) I uncovered an interesting pattern. I found those five questions, or some variation of them, are nearly always part of their thinking as they approach unbelievers:

1. HOW WOULD YOU DESCRIBE YOUR RELATIONSHIP WITH GOD?

The subject is best approached with one's using the word "God" instead of the word "Jesus." It is often less threatening for people to talk about God than to talk about Jesus. Satan seems to have geared people to shut us off when they hear the word "Jesus." So begin with "God."

Of course, some other circumstances will generally precede that first question. Sometimes God opens up opportunities for us when people make comments on national news items that are religious in nature. They may be impressed (or depressed) by some movie or TV program. Other times, the opener may be a book they have read or personal tragedy in their family or business. Still other times, it is possible to begin with a question like Betty used when she asked, "Do ya'll go to church?" The key is to pray for an open door (Colossians 4:3) and then be sensitive to God's working in people's lives. When we see God at work with our unbelieving friends through one of those things, we might ask them what they think God would say about it. Then we can proceed with the first of those regularly-used five questions.

2. HAS THAT RELATIONSHIP EVER COME TO THE PLACE WHERE YOU KNOW FOR SURE YOU WOULD GO TO HEAVEN IF YOU DIED?

To the question "Has your relationship with God come to the place where you know for sure you would go to heaven if you died?" it is common to add the phrase "or are you still on the way?" Some prefer to say, "If God were to ask you why He should let you into heaven, what would you say?" The point is, true believers are usually certain of their relationship with God. The Bible says, "The Spirit Himself bears witness with our spirit that we are children of God" (Romans 8:16). This question not only helps the Christian discern whether or not the one he is talking to is a believer, but it also helps the non-Christian to spotlight a specific shortcoming in his relationship with God.

3. DID YOU KNOW THE BIBLE SAYS YOU CAN KNOW FOR SURE?

Let them read 1 John 5:13. That verse not only shows "that you may *know* that you have eternal life," but also that this knowing is for those "who *believe* in the name of the Son of God (italics added)" That, then, leads naturally to the next question.

4. DO YOU KNOW WHAT IT MEANS TO BELIEVE?

Now show them John 1:12, explaining that *believe* means *receive*. An illustration is helpful here. For example, you can believe a certain medicine will help you, but until you take it (that is, receive it) your faith will not do you any good. Betty's example of receiving a pen is probably the best.

There are any number of ways you can illustrate this. Once while discussing it at a lunch with a man, I poured some coffee out of my cup onto the table just in front of him. Then I asked him if he believed the napkin I was holding could wipe it up before it ran onto his pants. He sat for a moment watching the spill get closer and closer to his lap, then answered, "No — yes — I don't know — give me that thing!" Then he grabbed the napkin and wiped up the stream of coffee before it spilled off the table onto his suit. I then explained how, of the four responses he made, three of them ("yes," "no," and "I don't know") were all useless faith. To respond, "Yes," to Christ is just as useless as to respond "No," or, "I don't know," if it does not involve receiving Him. The Bible says, "The demons also believe, and shudder" (James 2:19). The spilled coffee made clear to him that only when he received Christ like he received the napkin would his sins be wiped away.

5. WOULD YOU PRAY WITH ME TO RECEIVE JESUS CHRIST AS
YOUR SAVIOR RIGHT NOW?

It is best to invite a person to pray with you right then. I
have found that nearly 100 percent of those who say they will
pray later, do not. If the person insists on waiting, write out a
prayer on your business card and give it to him or her for a
reminder. Of course we must understand that praying a
prayer is not to be equated with receiving Christ. Neverthe-
less, a prayer can be an effective way of communicating that
decision to God.

Sue also offered four common last-minute objections to
receiving Christ. Here is a list of those with the answers Betty
gave.

Her first objection was, "I'd like to believe, but I have too
many doubts." That comment reveals a misunderstanding of
the John 1:12 idea of what it means to believe. Today we use
the word *believe* in two completely different ways. One is
to describe the opposite of doubt, and the other is to indicate a
decision. As Betty explained, biblical faith for salvation is a
decision to receive God's gift of eternal life. If faith were a
matter of achieving a certain amount of relative nondoubt, it
would be a work of man instead of a gift from God, and the
Bible clearly says it is not a work of man (Ephesians 2:8-9;
Titus 3:5).

Remember the man who had to deal with the coffee I
spilled on the table? His first three responses as to whether or
not the napkin would wipe it up ("yes," "no," and "I don't
know") were assuming a definition of faith that means relative nondoubt. Only when he said, "Give me that thing,"
and received the napkin did he apply the biblical idea of faith
in Christ. His doubts and his nondoubts were all together in
his response. He took the napkin, doubts and all. In just that
way Jesus Christ asks us to receive Him, doubts and all. He

begs us to come to Him just as we are. Many people have the idea that they need to clean up their act before they receive Christ. But *all* our righteousness is as filthy rags (Isaiah 64:6) — even our righteous attempts to achieve less doubt. So, biblically speaking, there is no such thing as *not being able* to believe due to doubts; there is only *refusing* to believe. The question is not ''Can you receive Christ?'' but ''Will you?''

A second common objection to making a decision is, ''I already did that when I was young.'' Many people in America have grown up in a situation that required some sort of religious action by its young people. We are confirmed or baptized; we are asked to come forward, stand up, raise a hand, go through a class. It is true that God can use such an occasion to bring kids to Himself. In many cases, though, it is only another of the many growing-up procedures we perform. It may be highlighted in our memory but still not be a time when we actually received Christ. When you talk to an adult who has gone through one of those ceremonies as a child and ask him to accept Christ, he is going to immediately search back through his mental file of religious memorabilia, desperately looking for something he can equate with what you are talking about. And, sure enough, most of us can find something. A normal response is, ''I've done that as a child.'' Be ready for it. The best answer is to go through the above reasoning with the person, especially if you, too, can recall such an experience, and then go on to ask him what he told God at that time. If (as is usually true) he doesn't remember, ask him to pray with you now to be sure.

A third last-minute holdout is a comment similar to, ''I pray all the time,'' or, ''I do that every night before I go to sleep.'' Not only is it true that many of us went through some childhood religious ceremony, but one other fact is true of almost all adults: they pray. From atheists to fanatics, most people pray. Also, realizing their imperfections, most people ask God to forgive their sins and accept them. And they do that regularly. The trouble is, Jesus Christ is the only solution for that.

Besides, God never forgives *sins* nor does He want us to ask Him to accept *us*. God forgives *sinners,* not sins. "Forgive *us* our debts" (Matthew 6:12, italics added) says the model prayer Christ gave His disciples. Sins must be paid for. Either we pay for them for eternity, or we receive Christ's payment for them on the cross; but they must be paid for, not just forgiven. So we need not ask Christ to accept us. Instead, *we* need to accept *Him.* The difference here goes far beyond semantics. People saying they do what we are talking about every night, do not understand what we are talking about.

A fourth typical response is, "For me this will be a long process of study." That is a response I would readily agree with. Then I would offer to meet with the person. There are several reasons. For one thing, a person becomes "born again" (in the sense of John 3:3 and 1 Peter 1:3-5) when he receives Christ, not necessarily when he prays a prayer to that effect. Try as we may not to manipulate a person into an insincere commitment, it happens. I do not find it uncommon to pray with a person to receive Christ two or three times — as his awareness begins to grow. Of course, you are born again at only one point in time, and salvation is not something you ooze into — it is a gift and you get it all at once. But just exactly *when* the person we are talking with makes that choice, we do not know. And that is not important. What is important is that he *does,* and the best way to make sure he does is to help him get regular input from the Bible.

Another reason I like the "further study" response is that it gives me an opportunity to pray with the person to receive the

Lord Jesus Christ as God's only means for a relationship with Himself. And that relationship is essential in order for God to teach him the Scriptures.

WHAT ABOUT SUE?

As we mentioned, Betty led Sue to Christ that day. But it did not end there. They began to meet together once a week to study the Bible — kids and all. It would have been easy to use their children as an excuse, and often it was difficult to concentrate, but they pressed on. Today Sue is a growing woman of God being a representative of Jesus Christ to her family.

12 • How Do We Know That God Exists?

"Turn around and go back!"

Steven began to argue with himself as he stopped and started on that parking lot Dallas calls Central Expressway. "You've sure got nerve! Who do you think you are? Can anybody convince a man like Bill that God exists? He owns and operates his own business. He's read a great deal in psychology and science. Besides, he has already thought this thing through."

Steve was scared.

The slow traffic gave him time to look at the drivers in the cars around him. He was sure none of them faced the threatening situation he did. "What lucky people," he thought. "I'm sure none of them are going any place where they'll have to prove God exists."

Once he finally left the expressway, finding Bill's office was easy. Too easy. Actually, Steve was hoping he would not be able to find it. If he could just get lost, he would have a good excuse to put off talking with Bill. But, no such luck. Or should I say, no such sovereignty of God. Anyway, there he was, knocking on the door of Bill's office.

Bill met him with a friendly smile and a firm handshake. Steve was quaking inside as he sat down. They had met the previous Monday night at a home discussion about life and

God. It had seemed so easy to strike up a conversation afterward and ask for this appointment.

But now that he was here sitting across the desk from his new acquaintance, Steve felt like he was on stage. He would have preferred to face an audience of a thousand people as long as they could not ask questions. Could he show God to Bill? Jesus said, "Peace I leave with you; My peace I give to you" (John 14:27), but right then it did not seem the southeast part of Dallas was included.

Bill's office was obviously that of a busy man, cluttered with papers and projects his manufacturing company was working on. The two men reviewed their discussion of the past Monday night. "I don't believe in a personal God," Bill repeated. "It seems more reasonable to believe that things evolved over a long period of time."

At that point, Steve had to choose between two routes. One would be to discuss evolution and argue that anyone who believed in it could not possibly believe in the Bible. But Jesus said that the seed (the Word of God) would develop best on softened soil (Mark 4:20). With some people evolution is an appropriate subject for discussion; but with Bill, it would only thicken the wall between them.

The other alternative was to find a way to scale the wall and see what it looked like from Bill's side. They needed to find an area of agreement to build on. His convictions about evolution gave Steve a narrow opening through which to get over to Bill's side. He was "interested" in believing whatever was most *"reasonable."*

"For a starter, let's come to terms with our purpose," Steve said.

"Well," Bill interjected, "isn't the purpose to prove God exists?"

"Of course," Steve concurred, "and we agree that the

underlying assumption we'll have in every judgment we make will be that it must be reasonable — right?''

"Oh — yeah — right!''

"Since we are attempting to prove God exists, we need to first talk about the words 'to prove' and then the words 'God exists.' ''

"Sounds good to me,'' Bill said, settling back in his chair and lighting a cigarette.

Steve ventured a bold statement. "You know, Bill, if anybody can tell me what his standard of proof is, I can prove 'God exists' using that standard.''

"What if I say I only believe what I can see?'' Bill responded.

"Oh, come on, Bill,'' Steve almost interrupted him. "Don't you believe in some things you can't see — like electricity? Love? Hate? Would it be reasonable to use two standards, one for proof of God and another for everything else?''

Bill took a long draw on his cigarette and nodded thoughtfully. As he reflected on that, he admitted he could not specify exactly what he *was* using as a basis for proof.

Steve suggested, "The reason we believe in the proof of the existence of electricity, love, and hate is not because we can see them, but because we can see their effects. Would you agree that every effect requires a cause?''

"Yes, of course,'' Bill responded. "That's a basic assumption of all science.''

"Then could we say that's the reason we believe in electricity? What I mean is: it's more reasonble to believe in it than not to believe in it as an explanation of why the lights go on when you flip the switch on the wall. Isn't the same thing true of love and hate? We can't see them, but we can see the kindnesses of love and the travesties of hatred.''

Bill nodded cautiously. Then he added, "But to tell you the truth, I need to see if that's really appropriate for the existence of God."

Steve aimed his cause-and-effect reasoning at three targets: the natural universe, the personalities in the universe, and the design of the universe.

"If I told you this building got here by the wind blowing it up off the Texas prairie and the squirrels putting it together, you wouldn't believe me, would you, Bill?"

"Nope."

"Why not?"

"Because that's impossible."

"But what you really mean is that the wind and the squirrels aren't a sufficient cause to produce this building as an effect. Right?"

"Of course."

Steve went on, "The universe is also an effect, but there is no observable cause sufficient to produce it."

"Why couldn't the universe be its own cause?" Bill asked, raising his eyebrows. (He had a habit of doing that when making a point he had thought about a lot.) Then he took a drink out of a huge glass of ice water and continued. "It seems just as reasonable to me to assume the universe made itself as to say God made it."

"The problem is," Steve reasoned, "the universe has never been observed doing that. It has never made something out of nothing."

"OK," Bill agreed, "but if God is the cause of the universe, don't we then need something else to make God? After all, God would be an effect which requires a cause."

"Yes. But God is different from the universe in one very significant way. Whereas the universe is not eternal, God is. Something somewhere has to be eternal, and cause-and-effect requires that something to be a some*one* — a personal God. Since God is eternal, we don't need to ask about His cause. How could anything eternal have a cause? By the way, the God described in the Bible is that kind of God."

"Couldn't we just consider God to be nature?" asked Bill.

"Oh, sure," Steve agreed. "You can use the word 'nature' instead of the word 'God,' but this nature-God must be a person."

"Why?" Bill asked. The studious expression on his face told Steve he was hoping for a definition of God that would somehow marry a belief in God with atheism.

"Well," Steve continued, "the universe we have contains people with personalities. By that I mean they have intellect, emotion, and will. And something impersonal like the universe has never been observed producing anything personal like people. Even statues and paintings that only depict personalities come from people who are at least personal. The impersonal marble never carves a statue, and the impersonal canvas never paints a painting. In the same way, if God wasn't at least a person, He would not be a sufficient cause to produce you and me."

"I guess I always thought that was the most reasonable," Bill admitted. "But I'm glad we could think it through."

"Design is the third effect that requires a cause," Steve ventured. "Can we talk about that a minute?"

"Sure." Bill's ashtray was filled with cigarette butts now, and the big glass of water was gone, leaving only some ice cubes on the bottom. He put one in his mouth. As his tongue wrestled with the ice, he mumbled, "What do you mean by design?"

"Just that no chance happening has ever produced anything comparable to a snowflake, a flower, or a living cell. We might as well ask, 'How long would you have to shake a box of radio parts before it assembled itself into a radio?' It never would, of course. All you'd get is a bunch of broken radio parts. In the natural universe, things always go from order to disorder, not the other way around. Does your office tend to get more or less orderly if you leave it alone?''

"But," Bill insisted, "they have done experiments where amino acids have formed which make up DNA and then protein. Isn't that the production of order and design?''

"Yes, but that's just the point. It took the intelligence of the experimenter setting up the experimental conditions just so and controlling it carefully. If they poured it all in a mud puddle out in the street or in a Mississippi swamp, it would never produce anything, no matter how long they watched it. The 'order' required the intelligence of man. All the observations we've ever made show that design comes from intelligent beings with a purpose. It's only reasonable that the universe isn't the only exception to the rule.''

Steve reached over to a piece of paper on Bill's desk and drew a circle with his pen. "Let's suppose this circle represents everything there is to know about everything. If you were to draw a circle within that circle that represents what you know, how big would it be?''

"Just a dot," Bill readily admitted. He immediately understood. If we deny the existence of God, then we are also saying we know everything there is to know. Since we do *not* know everything there is to know, God could be found outside of what we know. It is, therefore, not reasonable to claim we *know* God does *not* exist.

After a review of all the facts of this discussion, Bill concluded that they had proved God exists. Helping him examine his own position resulted in a softening of his heart that resulted in an openness to Steve — and eventually to God.

To Prove God Exists

Let us recap the stages that helped Bill move from atheism to agnosticism to belief in a personal God. There are many apologetic approaches to the existence of God. The discussion used here borrows from several, particularly those based on cause-and-effect reasoning. Here are four points to notice:

1. WHAT DO YOU MEAN BY "PROOF"?

To establish what is meant by "proof" is crucial because, although evidence is objective, proof is subjective. It is important to establish what the particular person you are reasoning with considers proof to be. That is as important for him as it is for you, because people usually do not know what their own standards are.

I recall a discussion I had with a man involved in one of the major cults. His cult believed Jesus was the Messiah but did not believe the Messiah was God. He told me if I could "prove" to him from the Bible that the Messiah was God, he would receive Him and reject the cult. "But I must first know how many verses constitute proof," I said, "else I could just keep giving you verses, and you could keep saying that it's not enough for proof." He decided on three. I showed him three verses that said the Messiah was God (Isaiah 7:14, Isaiah 9:6, and Matthew 1:23, as I recall), and after another half hour of reasoning, he prayed with me to receive Jesus Christ as his *God*.

If you do not know what definition of proof you are aiming at, your chances of hitting it are quite slim. In this case, Bill *thought* his standard was what he could see. So Steve had to point to electricity, love, and hate as examples of things he believed in that he could not see.

2. WHAT DETERMINES PROOF?

Epistemology, the study of knowing, asks questions like, "How do we know that what we think we know is real?" But for most people, it all boils down to simple cause-and-effect. If there is a house (an effect), then we can "know" there was someone who built it (a cause). Furthermore, we know that wind, rain, dirt, trees, and stones around it are not a sufficiently complex cause to explain the house as an effect. In other words, someone could prove to us how the house got there only if his reasoning was consistent with cause-and-effect. So we can generally establish cause-and-effect as the basic way people determine proof.

3. HOW DO WE KNOW GOD CAUSED IT ALL?

We can then proceed to the third point, which is that of determining that cause-and-effect shows it is reasonable to say God exists. To do that, we suggest that a personal God is the only reasonable cause for at least three effects: the natural universe, the personal beings within that universe, and the design of the universe.

As far as the universe itself is concerned, is it more reasonable to say it was produced by a God who could create than to suppose it came from nothing or made itself? The Mona Lisa is a great painting, but we don't conclude that the Mona Lisa painted itself. Rather, the existence of a Mona Lisa implies an artist who painted it. The Mona Lisa has never been observed painting anything. Neither has the universe ever been observed making something from nothing.

Furthermore, it makes more sense that there is an eternal God who always existed than to suppose the universe itself has always existed, because nothing *in* the universe is eternal. Since no part of it lasts forever, then it is only reasonable that all its parts put together were not there forever either.

Concerning personality, it is more true to cause-and-effect reasoning to say that humans, having personality, came from a personal God than to suppose they came from an impersonal universe. Everything reflecting personality comes from a personal being. Take the painting we mentioned above. Paintings often depict intelligence, emotion, or willful acts of people. Those are reflections of the personality of the painter. Because the works of art exist, we know the artist exists. So also the artist himself is a work of art reflecting the existence of personality in his Maker. So God must be at least personal.

When we consider the designs in the universe, we can see it is more consistent to assume they came from a God with a purpose for creating than to suppose they are chance happenings. Experience teaches us that things always go from order to disorder, unless an intelligent personality purposefully reverses the process. Radio, TV, and cars, as well as our houses and nearly everything in them, reflect the purposes of their designers. Besides that, they need to be maintained. Left to themselves, they break down and quit — which is true of our bodies, too. The universe is full of beauty and design, and our consistent observation is that beauty and design never happen by chance.

4. IS IT POSSIBLE TO KNOW GOD DOES NOT EXIST?

Steve and Bill agreed that it is not reasonable to say God could not exist. That followed from the argument that you would have to know everything there is to know in order to be sure that God could not exist. If you knew only a part, God might be known from another part.

All that led to the conclusion that the most "reasonable" decision is that a personal God does exist.

WHAT DO WE MEAN BY "GOD"?

It is common to find people who believe in the word "God." It is also increasingly common to find that many — probably most — of those same people who believe in something called "God" do not believe in a personal God. What I mean is: they do not believe in the existence of a real live person who created the universe and remains in sovereign control of it.

Hebrews 11:6 reads, "And without faith it is impossible to please Him, for he who comes to God *must believe that He is,* and that He is a rewarder of those who *seek Him,* italics added." In other words, the first step in coming to God is to understand that there is a real, personal, ultimately sovereign being to come to.

If we define an atheist as someone who does not believe in God as the Bible describes God, we would find most people are indeed atheists. Eastern mysticism, evolution, situation ethics, and the existential playboy philosophies all have contributed to a redefinition of the word "God."

When Thomas Altizer and others in the 1960s said that, "God is dead," they did not mean the God of the Bible had died. They meant that the word "God" is out-of-date. The *word* "God" died, or at least they believed it ought to. God as defined in the Bible, according to them, had never been alive.

In reality, the word "God" did not die. Instead, people kept on using it with new definitions. Those new definitions deny the existence of the sovereign creator the Bible describes. In other words, they describe a straw god to be burned at the discretion of the definer.

Our discussion was designed to bring about a rediscovery of the God who is.

WHAT ABOUT BILL?

What should we do when we meet someone like Bill? Cross the street and walk by on the other side? The Corinthians evidently thought so. Paul told them, "I wrote you in my letter not to associate with immoral people; I did not at all mean with the immoral people of this world, or with the covetous and swindlers, or with idolaters; for then you would have to go out of the world" (1 Corinthians 5:9-10).

Yet, what do we say to people like Bill? Tell them what the Bible says? That is often a good first step. Even people who do not believe the Bible can be convicted by it if they are willing to hear what it says (Isaiah 55:11). But that would not work with Bill. The Holy Spirit had not yet brought him to the place where he was ready to accept the Bible as God's Word or receive Jesus as God. That does not mean the Holy Spirit was not working on him. Bill was open to considering truth as long as he did not have to presuppose that God existed or that the Bible was right.

At the time of this writing, Bill and Steve are still meeting. After they had been getting together every week for one year and two months, Bill received Jesus Christ as his own God and Savior. They are now studying the Bible together. The same soil softening that brought him to a belief in God led him to a saving knowledge of God's Son and into a growing relationship with Him.

13 • Borrowed Wisdom

There are two characteristics of anything alive: it grows and it reproduces. The same is true of those who are alive spiritually. Reproduction of our faith in the Lord Jesus Christ is commanded in the Bible, but the commandment merely tells us to do what is normal to a living supernatural spirituality. When we have a new life in Christ, we naturally have an urge to reproduce.

But how? Just because something is natural does not mean it is always done well. Doing it well takes wisdom. As we look at the Word of God and the way God has reproduced it most effectively in the lives of people, we can learn to be sharper instruments in God's hand.

This chapter does not contain everything you will ever need to know about witnessing. What I *have* included here are some ideas that one person (without the spiritual gift of evangelism or a natural gift of gab) had to learn the hard way.

THE PRIORITY OF UNBELIEVER FRIENDSHIPS

Our peer group exerts tremendous influence over the way we think — even as adults. We feel comfortable thinking thoughts and living life-styles similar to the ones around us. Those thoughts can become thought-habits that we believe without thinking.

For example, people from different parts of the world see

things in unique ways. Various areas of our own country tend toward similarity. There's a "Noo Yawk" life-style, a California mentality, Southern hospitality. Living in Dallas, I feel good about being a Cowboy fan. But of course I am surrounded by over a million other Cowboy fans. I feel good about flying because I hang around with other guys who fly. As the saying goes, "If you've seen one, you've seen them all." People feel good about developing beliefs and habit-patterns similar to those around them — their peer group.

Unbelievers, like the rest of us, often feel "right" about their belief or disbelief because it is in harmony with those of the people around them. Like the rest of us, they feel comfortable when their life-styles and belief patterns reach a functioning status quo with those closest to them.

One of the best ways to penetrate that pattern is friendship. Suppose we think of witnessing as building a friendship that may result in a decision for Christ, instead of aiming for a decision that could result in a friendship. Then Christianity could infect the life of almost anybody! A Christian who is a close friend of an unbeliever becomes *part of* his peer group. The thoughts of the unbeliever then must change to accommodate those of his new Christian friend. After a time, the non-Christian's value system becomes less comfortable to him and he begins to feel better about considering the biblical ideas of his Christian friend.

The Holy Spirit often uses such relationships to reveal the glory of God to the unbeliever through the changed life of his Christian friend. Reflecting on the way he reached the Thessalonians, the apostle Paul wrote, "Having thus a fond affection for you, we were well-pleased to impart to you not only the gospel of God but also our own lives, because you had become very dear to us" (1 Thessalonians 2:8).

Suppose our eternal reward in heaven depends on how

many unbelieving friends we have? Of course, it doesn't —
at least not exclusively. But consider that. When Paul talked
about rewards in 2 Corinthians 5:10, he went on to say,
"Therefore knowing the fear of the Lord, we persuade men"
(v. 11). And when he discussed rewards in 1 Corinthians
9:17-18 he went on to say, "I have become all things to all
men, that I may by all means save some" (v. 22). And the
way he went about saving some in Thessalonica was through
building friendships. Friendships can be the key that unlocks
the hearts of those around us.

FRIENDSHIP IS A NATURAL FOLLOW-UP

Every so often somebody will do a survey and publish
some statistics about evangelism. Those statistics always
vary, but I have noticed one fairly consistent pattern. There is
a big gap between the number who claim to have made a
decision for Christ and the number who go on to grow in the
Lord in some measurable way. There may, of course, be all
kinds of reasons for that; but one fact is sure. Almost everybody seems to have a problem with follow-up.

I have also noticed that, of the people whom we have seen
come to Christ over the last ten years or so, from 80 to 90
percent go on to grow in the Lord. I do not mean just the ones
I have led to Christ. I mean those I have known about — like
the ones in this book. What is the difference? Friendship! I
have also noticed that when someone makes a further survey
of how those people who do go on in Christ came to be saved,
it is almost always through close friends or relatives —
someone close to them who cared enough.

SOME FRIENDSHIP PATTERNS

The Bible is packed full of friendships. God has chosen to
reveal Himself by bringing one person up alongside another

so closely that one becomes infected with the glory of God as it radiates from the other. There were Elijah and Elisha (1 Kings 19:19-21); Eli and Samuel (1 Samuel 3:1-19); Moses and Joshua (Joshua 1:1-3); Naomi and Ruth (Ruth 1:15-18); Mary and Elizabeth (Luke 1:39-45); Christ and the twelve, especially Peter (John 21:15); Luke and Theophilus (Luke 1:1-4, Acts 1:1-2); Peter and John Mark (1 Peter 5:13); Peter and Silvanus (1 Peter 5:12); Barnabas and John Mark (Acts 15:39); Barnabas and Paul (Acts 11:22-26; 13:2); Paul and Silas (Acts 15:40); Paul and Timothy (Acts 16:1-3); Paul and Titus (Titus 1:4); Paul and Philemon (Philemon 4, 13, 14, 17, 20); Paul and Onesimus (Philemon 10-11); Paul and Archippus (Colossians 4:17); Paul and Prisca and Aquila (2 Timothy 4:19); Paul and Onesiphorus (2 Timothy 4:19); Paul and Eubulus (2 Timothy 4:21); Paul and Pudens (2 Timothy 4:21); Paul and Linus (2 Timothy 4:21); Paul and Claudia (2 Timothy 4:21); Paul and Trophimus (2 Timothy 4:20); Paul and Erastus (2 Timothy 4:20); Paul and Zenas (Titus 3:13); Paul and Apollos (Titus 3:13); Paul and Epaphras (Philemon 23); John and Gaius (3 John 1); John and Demetrius (3 John 12); and many others.

Making friends is not the only way to witness. And if it is done as a gimmick, it will be manipulative and phony. But when we sincerely want to be people's friends whether they receive Christ or not, we give them a great opportunity to see what the living God can do with plain old unfancy sinners like us.

LOTS OF LITTLE THINGS

After years of studying people who are more gifted than I at relating their faith to unbelievers, I have picked up lots of pointers that all add up to successful witnessing. A few of those little gems are:

1. If you are talking with someone you will probably see again (a neighbor, relative, or business associate), *it is usually better not to attempt to lead him to Christ during the first discussion about spiritual things.* The word "usually" is, of course, important. A person may be ready, and if he is, you must be available to explain the whole plan of salvation and invite him to receive Christ. But by and large it is better to let your friend absorb the truth over several conversations.

2. *If possible, talk with people alone.* An unbeliever generally finds considering new issues easier without an audience. If there is another believer present, your friend may be tempted to debate instead of decide. If you are with another unbeliever, your friend may think about agreement instead of truth.

3. *Realize that rejection is an essential part of acceptance.* People tend to deal with any new idea by first rejecting it. If they don't reject it, then either it is not new or they are not really considering it. After rejecting an idea, they are open to reconsidering it; that second stage in people's thinking involves accepting part of the new idea and rejecting other parts. Then finally they are open to accepting the idea. The progression may take minutes or years. I especially remember one time when I told this to a group of Christians. Two weeks later one man came up to me and said, "You know, when you first said that, I thought it was absolutely wrong. Then I thought about it and realized that it was probably partly true. Now I tend to think you're right."

People who witness successfully realize the importance of rejection. If we do not establish a rejection, then we will probably get a dead-end answer when we ask people to receive Christ. They may say, "Oh, I've already done that" or "I do that every day" or "I've always believed, why should I decide that now?" On the other hand, if we have allowed our friend to establish a rejection — like one of the twelve questions mentioned in this book — then he has an opportunity to realize his need to make a decision.

4. *"Pray without ceasing"* (1 Thessalonians 5:17). This is not a "little thing." I mention it briefly only because this is not a book on prayer. But it is prayer that effects a super- natural work. Mature men and women of God have *always* been people of prayer. All the friends and all the right techniques and all the right answers to all the questions will not put spiritual life into anybody. God can and will use us as instruments in His hand. It is true that all those things can make us sharper and therefore more useful instruments. But it is God who causes the growth (1 Corinthians 3:6-7).

Man can build a statue, but he cannot make it breathe. He can paint a painting, but he cannot make it live. We can build churches, have evangelistic campaigns, or try to reach our neighbors. But unless God is in it, those activities are worth- less. And the divine means of effecting any supernatural work is prayer. "The effective prayer of a righteous man can accomplish much." And you know who said that? The man who probably knew our Lord better than anyone else — His physical half-brother, James, in 5:16 of his epistle.

5. *Be familiar with references that quote Jesus Christ directly,* not that Jesus' words are any more inspired than the rest of the Bible (2 Timothy 3:16), but unbelievers are often more curious about what Jesus said. Skeptics have fostered the idea that the Christianity we believe was made up by His followers. It is common to hear, "Well, *Jesus* never claimed to be God or the only way. That was just made up later on." The gospel of John is especially valuable here — I consider it God's manual on salvation. Here are some passages you should be familiar with. I generally take a new believer through these passages as soon as possible if I have not

already covered them with him before he receives Christ.
They include: John 3:16-18, 36; 4:25-26; 5:24; 6:28-29;
8:24; 10:10, 28-29; 14:1-9; and 20:26-29.

6. *Emphasize biblical understanding.* Many well-
meaning believers fail in their attempts to witness to friends
because they require them to believe the Bible without giving
them a chance to understand it. I recently asked a Hindu
gentleman, "Do you understand what the Bible says about
God?"

"I don't believe what the Bible says," he returned.

"Oh, I know," I continued. "That's why I didn't ask you
if you believe it but if you understand it."

"Well, no, not really," he readily admitted.

"Wouldn't it be more reasonable to understand something
before you decide not to believe it?" I suggested.

He agreed. "I never really thought about it that way," he
said.

As a result of that conversation, he began attending a study
put on by a good Bible-oriented church in the Dallas area.

God promised that His Word would not return without
accomplishing what He desired (Isaiah 55:11). The Bible is
the sword of the Christian (Ephesians 6:17). If your only
weapon in a battle was a sword, and your adversary did not
believe in swords, would you put it down and admit defeat? I
hope not! If you use it, he'll believe it! In Thessalonica as
well as in Rome, Paul "reasoned with them from the Scriptures" (Acts 17:2), "trying to persuade them concerning
Jesus, from both the Law of Moses and from the Prophets"
(Acts 28:23).

Many of the people to whom we witness reject the Bible
without having the foggiest notion about its real message.
You may have noticed that in the discussions recorded in this
book. Often faith in Jesus Christ merely awaits a clarification

of what the Bible really says.

7. *Be a student of unbelievers.* You cannot learn to answer unbeliever's questions by simply studying a book — even this one. It is important to learn from books, other people, sermons, seminars, or anywhere you can, but be sure you think the answers through *yourself.* Every personality is different, and some answers will be more useful to you than others.

After you have learned some sound biblically logical answers and then thought them through by yourself, try them out on some non-Christian friends. Do *not* try your answers out on other Christians.

Have you ever been in Christian groups that were going to discuss questions they have been asked by non-Christians? They are often not the questions unbelievers would ask, and believers and unbelievers are usually not satisfied by the same answers. We find that Christians get all excited about answers the non-Christians could care less about. And when we give answers that *have* proved to be effective with unbelievers for years, many Christians say, "You'd never convince an unbeliever with that!"

If you want to reach unbelievers, then you must study the minds of unbelievers. Try out your answers on *them.* Most people are very willing to be helpful. Just honestly tell some unbelieving friend that you have been studying some questions and answers and you would like his opinion about them.

8. *Encourage conversation.* Often an unbeliever has been run over, somewhere in life, by a religious steamroller. Nearly three thousand years ago Solomon wrote, "He who gives an answer before he hears, It is folly and shame to Him," and also, "A brother offended is harder to be won than a strong city, and contentions are like the bars of a castle" (Proverbs 18:13, 19). Anything that resembles man-

ipulation or a lecture series may ring in the unbeliever's ears like the rumble of another approaching steamroller.

But Solomon also wrote, "A man has joy in an apt answer, and how delightful is a timely word!" (Proverbs 15:23). One excellent way to find that "apt answer" is to listen. Encourage conversation. How? Ask for opinions instead of facts. Facts are threatening. Opinions are exciting. If we ask rhetorically, "What did Jesus say about that?" we may be setting up the person for our answer (which no one likes) or requiring him to be knowledgeable about what Jesus said. Because he is probably not an expert on Jesus, we have placed him in an embarrassing position. Ask instead, "What do you think about the statement Jesus made when He said . . . ?" Then quote it or let your friend read it. That way he has the freedom to deal with the truth in a way most familiar to him — his own opinion.

Another way to encourage conversation is to let the person challenge what *you* believe. The statement "If the Bible is full of errors — show me one" says you want to show your doubting friend how ignorant he is and how smart (or how much of a smart-aleck) you are. It is better to say something like, "I've come to believe that the Bible does not have any errors in it. I don't want to believe that if it's not true for everybody. Does that seem reasonable to you?"

Our conversation should always be motivational. When the Lord Jesus spoke with unbelievers, some were excited, some were outraged, but nobody was bored! Paul told the Colossians, "Conduct yourselves with wisdom toward outsiders, making the most of the opportunity. Let your speech always be with grace, seasoned, as it were, with salt, so that you may know how you should respond to each person" (Colossians 4:5-6).

BE HONEST TO GOD

It is tempting to pretend that God never said "Go therefore and make disciples of all the nations" (Matthew 28:19). But He did.

Take me, for instance. After more than ten years of work in evangelism, I am as convinced as ever that I do *not* have the gift of evangelism. And my tendency is to use that as an excuse to pretend God did not say what He did.

I remember one time feeling sufficiently guilty for not witnessing. I crammed my pockets full of tracts, cornered some guy, and dumped the whole load on him. I embarrassed him and humiliated myself. My victim fled, and I retreated to my room with my theological tail between my legs.

"I'll be a teacher," I thought. "After all, the need for teaching is almost epidemic in Christianity today." Do we need good teachers? Of course we do. Did I have the gift of teaching? Probably so. What does that have to do with the fact that God left me on this earth to tell others? Nothing. It was just my way of explaining to God that He really didn't say what He did. All my attempts at rationalizing did not change the fact that there is "more joy in heaven over one sinner who repents, than over ninety-nine righteous persons who need no repentance" (Luke 15:7). That hounded me. Even if I became a great teacher, I still must answer the question, "What difference will it make five hundred years from now?"

There are many gifts and many callings within the body of Christ, but none of them give us a license to neglect the lost. God does not want us to be something we cannot be. Nor does He want us to be oddballs. We just need to come to Him honestly, available (as 1 Corinthians 9:22 says) to become all things to all men, that we might by all means save some.